FRAGMENTS
OF
FRENCH

*An Unexpected Journey
of the Heart*

WANDA ST. HILAIRE

Destinations
Extraordinaire

Calgary, Alberta

Fragments of French
An Unexpected Journey of the Heart
Copyright © 2019 Wanda St. Hilaire. All Rights Reserved.

Published by Destinations Extraordinaire.
ISBN 978-1-894331-15-9 (print)
ISBN 978-1-894331-16-6 (digital)

Edited by Marie Beswick-Arthur.

Front cover art, "Oracles of Nature" © Francis A. Willey.
www.franciswilley.com

Cover design, titles, and layout by Ryan Fitzgerald.

www.wandasthilaire.com
www.fragmentsoffrench.com
www.lifebyheart.wandasthilaire.com
www.imsorryitscancer.com
destinoex@aol.com

First Edition

Printed and bound in Canada

About the Cover

IT WAS 2012. WORKING AT MY WRITING CAFÉ, I WAS SEATED next to an eclectic couple, both busy on their Macs. A haunting piano composition coming from their table disrupted my focus. I had been to Italy a year earlier, and it evoked a powerful flashback to a rainy night in Venice. Beautiful music from inside a mask maker's shop drifted out onto the canals, and my travel mate and I were drawn in by the piece. I knew I *needed* to have the music—so reminiscent of Italy—that my café neighbor was playing.

I asked who the composer was; Francis A. Willey, said it was his own. We met the following week for my CD purchase. For me, it was platonic love at first chat.

During our meeting, I learned that Francis was a fine art photographer who had recently won a Lucy Award, Fine Art Nude, in Los Angeles, and my sister and I, taken with his story, bought three exquisite pieces to contribute to the trip to Los Angeles. He has been exhibited, published, and internationally awarded, and is frequently published by Vogue.

Francis is a sensitive old-soul who prolifically creates photography, composes music and poetry, and is currently pursuing film. We have been friends since that day we met in the café. A true artist deeply dedicated to the world of art, he reminds me to never give up on my art—no matter the outcome.

Having Francis' photography on the cover of *Fragments of French* is an honor and an inspiration.

Oracles of Nature, 2016
This 35mm color film image conveys the feminine as the oracle, the sister, the ghost, the warrior, and the elemental grandeur.

The *Oracles of Nature* series pays tribute to the divine woman, an indispensable condition of the highest beauty.

Francis A. Willey
www.franciswilley.com

For my dear sister, whose unconditional and inexhaustible love has carried me through countless storms. I am unsure if she came to me in this lifetime as my gift, or I her penance.

Lana, I love you beyond measure.

♥

To Dolores
the rest of the
Story ... for
a long night
with a glass
of wine ♡

Wanda
A. Hilair
2020

Each of us views the world with a unique filter created by our upbringing, our past experiences, our hurts, and our pleasures. All events and people in this book are real—as seen from my perspective. Some names have been changed to protect the innocent, and the not so innocent.

For me, life without music is not life. The following **YouTube playlist** was my background soundtrack in the era of *Fragments of French*. I have created it to accompany the book. YouTube, Wanda St. Hilaire, Fragments of French:

https://tinyurl.com/y5cgjtjt
(No ads have been placed by author.)

In the back of this book you will find a **Language Glossary**. After that, you will also find a **Cast of Characters**, all real. In the event that you are interested in the current lives of the various characters peppered throughout the book, a brief overview is included.

The bestselling companion book of poetry written during this experience, *Of Love, Life and Journeys,* is available in a fresh, new second edition format on Amazon.

Thank you for joining me on this intimate journey ...

Wanda

Contents

FRAGMENTS
OF
FRENCH

*An Unexpected Journey
of the Heart*

1996

TWO OVERSIZED SUITCASES, A HANDBAG, AND A COUPLE OF worn leather totes sit in a tidy row beside a sleeping bag on the living room floor. The basement, which was filled with a lifetime of *tchotchkes*, is empty. The upstairs—the space of my rose-coloured sanctuary—is dismantled. Most of the furniture has been sold, and what is left is tucked and locked into storage bin #222. Even the keys to my glossy eggplant, prettiest-ever car are gone; a new owner has adopted her. All that remains in this two-story house are the suitcases I stare at on the floor.

I am at last alone, after a whirlwind of preparation, celebration, and farewells. My final guests, my parents, have reluctantly left me after a paralyzing phone call from afar. It was not easy for them to walk away, for an indeterminate amount of time, from a forlorn daughter about to fly off in a dumbfounded mess.

Our day-to-day lives typically flow with the minutiae of the known. There is the mundane and the comfortable; like the ratty robe that we wrap around ourselves to watch movies in, with a hot cup of tea from our favorite mug. There are our unvarying routines, our jobs, the people we know, and the places we frequent, which give us stability and a sense of certainty in an uncertain world.

And occasionally, there are the extraordinary moments when a life-altering fork in the road appears, when constancy vanishes underneath us and we are presented with an opportunity that excites us, stretches us far beyond the boundaries of our self-imposed restrictions, and scares the bejesus out of us. We have the freedom to choose, but we cannot know the long-term ramifications, or predict the final outcome of either decision, be it yay or nay.

Had I picked the road most traveled, this house would look the same as it did three months ago. My heartbeat would be steady and, at this moment, I would be asleep in my big brass bed, safely tucked under a thick, goose-down duvet. Monday morning, I would awaken to a flurry of faxes and phone calls in the small office upstairs, and then race off on a snowy road-trip for a week of intensive work. But that pathway may have led me to a deep gorge of regret, and a lifetime of what-ifs. I could not take that chance, ending up an old, disenchanted woman, retelling what might have been.

No one I know has done this before; I have no frame of reference. I am taking the fork to the far left, one that holds an exciting adventure fraught with potential peril. I have overcome my fears by nullifying them one by one. I am leaping without a net.

I crawl into my sleeping bag and toss restlessly, a barrage of questions battering my bewildered brain. I will leave tomorrow on a jet plane for the most unknown journey of my life. I do not know what awaits me, and I do not know when I will be back again.

ONE
PORTUGAL

When Lisbon Conspired

June / Junho

Love is an irresistible desire to be irresistibly desired.
—Robert Frost

"*Obrigado*," I say, the only Portuguese word I know, as I pay the airport cabbie. I have arrived in Lisbon on a humid June evening, at a small corner hotel on a noisy street not far from the center. Today is a national holiday and celebrations are underway.

Portugal is my second solo sojourn overseas. After facing my mortality head on, I vowed to myself that I would be true to my biggest *joie de vivre*—travel—and do it as much as possible. Two years ago, on a trip to the Greek Isles with a friend who was in the middle of a marital crisis, I spent the third week alone, happily loitering on the whitewashed island of Mykonos, and then navigating smog-ridden Athens. Last year, I shored up my courage and conquered my fears of traveling alone for my next adventure. Spontaneously booking a flight, I hopped a plane, without a map or a raincoat, for my dream destination—Italy. But that is an entirely different story.

Checking in, I drop my bags in the tiny room, and then venture out to investigate the festivities. Savory scents waft from under a sign that reads '*Petiscos*,' and the bright colors blur, as butterflies twirl in my stomach in this large, foreign city.

Coming to Lisbon was a decision based on the playful inner debate of a newly single, red-blooded woman: go to France and meet amorously-famed Frenchmen, or return to Portugal to experience it from a vastly different angle, and possibly discover the world of swarthy Mediterranean men.

My honeymoon on the Portuguese Algarve and Spanish Costa del Sol, seven years ago, was a month of newly wedded bliss. My husband and I leisurely traveled up and down the coastline, and then traversed the mountainous cliffs of Spain, into Sevilla and Granada—wandering gypsies with nothing more to concern ourselves with than which bottle of red to crack, and what hotel would meet the requirements of our rigorous romancing. Such a sweet, delicious beginning, yet so short lived.

Portugal won out after perusing the book *Wild Planet!* I learned that the month I wanted to travel in would be festival time here.

The sun is setting on Avenida da Liberdade, a wide, tree-lined boulevard teeming with thousands of Lisboans. I am in a space of duality as I maneuver through the throng; half of me is brave-hearted adventuress, the other half quakes and questions my sanity for again crossing an ocean alone. I restlessly weave in and out of the crush to observe the events, but I am soon overcome with exhaustion from the long flight.

I fall asleep on the hard twin bed to dream about wild stallions running on the red cliffs of the Algarve, lulled into a deep slumber by the white noise of a warm European night.

My internal time clock askew, I awaken before dawn, eager to investigate Lisbon. With only one night booked in this over-priced hotel, I will search for another room in the heart of the city. Taking my breakfast and a frothy cappuccino on a vine-shaded terrace, I then wander the busy streets. I find a suitable room that is antiquated and stark, but larger than any of the others. Although I don't need space, I like it. Retrieving my bags, I make my way back to the *pensão* near Rossio, the center of the action. The rotund owner is a cheery and welcoming man, and I feel that I am in safe hands.

Collapsing on the small bed, I find the room warmed by the unseasonably high temperature today. I daydream about what I shall do on this trip, my brain swinging from thought to thought. Slowly, my monkey mind settles into meditation. Relaxed, I drift into a blurry theta state.

Like a bud unfurling, an intense longing begins to push its way up my body and into my consciousness. Forming a prayer, I am cognizant of its power—a force that can be generated only from fervent desire and clear intent, unified in a deeply contemplative state. I pray that I will meet a man—not a typical holiday fling soon forgotten—but a real romance.

A man who will rock my world.

Single again for just over two years, when my husband left, the pain literally crippled me. Married only forty-two months, I loved him with every fiber of my being—and I know he loved me—but, for the sake of my sanity, I gave him an ultimatum: alcohol or me. Each week, as the deadline I'd set for a decision approached, I asked: "which will it be?" Each week the answer remained the same: "both."

The morning after he left, I lay immobilized: I could not get out of bed. It was the oddest sensation—and wildly frightening. I assumed a disc issue had flared, but from what, I didn't know. The chiropractor, who made an unprecedented house call, examined me, and then gently asked what was happening in my life. He listened and nodded.

"I'm afraid you have hysterical paralysis. It appears to be from emotional shock."

In that moment, my body had stopped for my broken heart. Now, here in Lisbon, I long for connection once again, and for what was stolen from me by the bitch-seductress, addiction.

Floating into a soft, euphoric nap, I awaken as the sun is setting. The pink light of dusk gives the shabby room a little forgiveness.

I shower, dress, and take paper and postcards down to the Baixa (By-sha), a colorful walking street filled with alluring shops, outdoor bars, and restaurants. At a busy bar, I purchase a half bottle of *vinho tinto*, and settle into writing under one of the many yellow and white striped umbrellas outside.

Scanning the café and Baixa, I consider whom I will first write to. Two men sit nearby, each alone. One is olive-skinned, attractive, and likely Portuguese. The other is a little older, early salt-and-pepper-flecked hair, lean, and lightly tanned. He too is handsome, and we lock eyes for a moment. Savoring a long sip of the wine and the buzz that is building, I begin my letters.

A glass later, I make direct eye contact with him again. Under the influence of the warm evening, the robust Douro wine, and this pretty street café, my body loosens. True to my sun sign, I live to be surrounded by all things foreign; these are the moments I impatiently await, and are quite possibly the only reason I get up for work every day.

The olive-skinned man adjusts his slackened tie, and gathers his briefcase and jacket to leave. Again, I catch Salt & Pepper's eye. Poker-faced, I secretly summon. Ever the storyteller, I return to my writing, and become engrossed in a new missive to my friend Monique in Paris. Finishing the last of my wine, I look up.

He is gone.

The night is still young, but I am disappointed. I wanted to meet this man, and I should have done something—smiled encouragingly or said hello. Packing up my things, I head toward the room.

At the edge of the Baixa I stop. Left or right? Either will take me back to my *pensão*. Peculiarly, I contemplate this. Right it is.

The evening is muggy and the area is humming. An old man is busking; singing a soulful ballad, as a group hypnotically encircles him. I negotiate through a mob of both tourists and locals; momentarily, I freeze. I spot him over the masses. Salt-and-Pepper, oh so tall and striking, is walking toward me.

Say something.

He walks past me.

Say something! Anything!

I start to a light tap on my shoulder.

"*Parlez-vous français, mademoiselle?*" he says with a smile that turns my insides upside down.

"*Un petit peu,*" I smile back, and gesture 'a little' with my thumb and forefinger.

"Would you like to go for a drink?" he says, again in French, but I understand with clarity.

"*Oui. Mais oui,*" I reply without hesitation.

Finding a noisy tent that has been set up as a makeshift bar for the multitude of festivals, we enter, lured by the revelry. Everyone here is Portuguese except us. We sit side-by-side and drink wine and listen to the music and my head swirls with the close proximity of this man.

Jean-François tells me that he speaks almost no English, but I couldn't care one fig; the challenge excites me all the more. As we attempt to converse, I pull all of the dusty French files from the far corners of my memory. His big energy is palpable and intoxicates me more than the alcohol.

After an indeterminate amount of wine, we collude in a plan to find the castle. One can see it clearly from the street, but the path to get there is not as simple as it would seem. Following arrows made from red Christmas lights, we slowly work our way up, up, up the hill, laughing all the way. How can this be so difficult?

Eventually, we abort the plan, and he suggests we wait for another day.

Even though we are now far from my *pensão*, we leisurely wind our way back, breaching the language barrier with a bizarre ease, one reserved for the universal language of love between journeyers.

Asking my travel agent his thoughts on Lisbon before I left, his bland response was, "It's just another big European city." Walking through this medieval neighborhood in the wee hours of the morning, I beg to differ, finding its antiquity and intrigue endearing.

There are many flavors of kisses: the lip-curling, repulsive, you-will-never-kiss-me-again-as-long-as-we-both-shall-live kiss; the perfunctory good night kiss; the peck-on-the-cheek; the short, but sweet kiss; the desperate attack kiss; the tongue-darting lizard lick; the mmmm-I-want-more-of-that kiss—but as he says good-night at the doorway of my *pensão*, he gives me the mother of all kisses: the Grande Dame—the movie-moment kiss—angels dancing on my tongue, a waterfall of oxytocin washing over me, my knees deliciously weak.

I fall asleep knowing there is no way we will not see each other tomorrow.

Giddy, I awaken already excited for my dinner date this evening with *le Français*, Jean-François. Not much else electrifies me more than the first flush, the anticipation of what could be, of what might happen in the mysterious realm of lust and love. Coupled with foreign love, it gets no better.

First order of the day, I find a small bookstore and purchase a pocket-sized French-English dictionary. After a light breakfast in Rossio, I hop the train to check out the city's beach. A weekday, the shoreline—a long, skinny strip of sand on the Tagus River—is active, but not busy. It is not the ocean, but still, it is a beach. It's cooler today, and I lazily read, have lunch, meander, and read more.

Numerous couples engage in various forms of play and love-making at the park by the train stop. Uninhibited in their actions, I smile as I observe their ardent displays. I love their liberation. '*Viva l'amor!*' my senses scream. My culture does not allow for this. 'Get a room!' is the common response to overt public displays of affection. We abhor physical passion that isn't concealed and contained.

Anxious to get back to my room, I board the train to prepare for my date.

On time to the minute, Jean-François arrives with another of his beguiling smiles, defusing my normal defenses. He leans down to kiss each cheek, and smells like fresh laundry and the forest. The scent of a man can instantly kill any interest or drive me wild. His is the latter.

We walk to a quaint downtown café he has chosen. I am neither small nor tall, but when a man can make me feel petite by his stature, it activates my all-girl self.

Too noisy to get his story last night, we fall into a deep conversation in this quiet café. He is an engineer who has worked two and a half decades for a large, worldwide company and is on contract with a national Portuguese corporation in Lisbon. He has been living here for three months, with one more month left in his term.

He orders in Portuguese: *bacalhau* for himself, and for me, a traditional pork dish. Speaking fondly of his teenage son, he is going through what sounds like a drawn out and unpleasant divorce. It does not occur to me that one should not get too deeply involved with a man embroiled in nasty divorce proceedings. He loves to laugh and is funny, even with the dictionary in hand. Touching my arm frequently, his manner of speech is animated and passionate.

It is now that he tells me he had been halfway to his *pensão* last night when he decided that he must return to the Baixa to find me. He says he is thrilled that he saw me on the street and did not lose me in the crowds of Lisbon. From the Alsace-Lorraine region of France, his accent and French words seduce me beyond measure. The irony of finding a Frenchman in Portugal, after my great debate, does not escape me.

We return to the Baixa for drinks al fresco. A light wind blows tonight, and my dress swirls and curls around my legs. My hair flies in my face and he pulls it back, fingers brushing softly across my cheek. A shiver rushes down my spine with this most intimate of touches: a gentle caress on one's face.

We talk and laugh into the night. Taking my hand, we begin to walk, and as we pass my street and onward to where I am sure he lives, there is no question in my mind, no hesitation. There is no need to discuss or ask.

Entering the darkened doorway of an old tenement building, we step into an antiquated cage-style elevator. His room faces onto a narrow courtyard with clothes drying on a multitude of crisscrossing lines. It is small, and cramped with his life of the past few months. His clothes, fresh from the launderer, are crisply folded and piled atop the armoire.

I sit on the edge of the bed and he leans down to kiss me, pressing into my body as I fall back. His kisses are firm, and his mouth tastes ever so slightly of the tiramisu we shared earlier. He slips off my dress with one move, his hands squeezing curves. Desire permeates every cell in my body, tickling each follicle. I lay breathless.

As his arms envelop me, I command time to stop. I want to lock into this mellifluous moment forever. Not knowing if it exists, or if it is only a figment of the collective imagination, this is the feeling I have yearned for and imagined many times. His kisses continue on in a sweet stretch, and to my surprise, it does exist.

Unhurried, his lovemaking is exquisite, true to the reputation of his countrymen. He kisses my forehead, my eyes, my cheeks, and the corners of my mouth, and then slowly down my body. Large hands explore, and mine are woven into his hair. His fingers tease the lines of my legs, and his lips move down my body, creating a red ripple of ache and delight.

Surrendered, I am as soft as a bed of down. The fragrant lavender on the bedside table further coaxes me to succumb, wholly, completely. I cling, his body sinking into mine. He is my familiar.

Gripping my hands, he holds them at my sides, pressing tightly. Tears sting my eyes, slowly rolling from my temples and dotting the pillow.

Sacred sweetness.

With French words tickling my ears, and feathery kisses teasing at my neck, my body undulates, repeatedly, following his deep rhythm, drinking in his intensity. I almost dissolve and disappear in the denouement.

He captures something inside of me, something that until now has not been bound or taken. This unrecognizable sensation feels strange—even outlandish—yet I have the unmistakable knowing that something has altered within, profoundly, swiftly.

I fall asleep with strong arms wrapped around me for the entirety of the night, the soothing sounds of Lisbon in the distance.

Awakened from liquid dreams to the hazy honey of early morning *faire l'amour*, there is no trace of awkwardness between us.

I find that my dress has been neatly hung, although when I do not know. I will be mildly presentable for my walk back to the *pensão*.

After his shower, Jean-François invites me to join him at a nearby café he visits each morning before work. He looks squeaky clean and refreshed. We pass a tiny desk in the dim hallway, and a smiling, motherly landlady pops out from a doorway, insistent on meeting me. Although this short conversation is in French and Portuguese, it is clear that she is pleased for Jean-François to have found a woman, and I can see that she has adopted him as one of her own.

The noisy *pâtisserie* has standing-room-only at the bar, typical for a busy European weekday. Jean-François orders a double espresso and two *pains au chocolat*, and I my daily cappuccino. The baker pulls a fragrant tray of freshly baked pastries from an oven directly in front of us. As I bite into my croissant, the chocolate still hot and velvety and running down my fingers, I cannot know that this is a moment I will never forget, and one I will seek to relive, to re-taste.

He draws me a map of the way back to Rossio on a small blue napkin, and I leave him only after he boards the bus. Passing businessmen in tailored suits and starched white shirts, I observe the workaday life of the Lisboans from my wistful world, a million miles away from my everyday life—energized by the tender night, twitterpated by the possibility of love, and high on travel. On the way, I plan for a daytrip to Sintra by train today.

The owner is picking up scattered leaves and sweeping the front stoop when I arrive at my room. Scratching at his heavy moustache, he smiles, and comments approvingly on the notion that I have already been out for an early morning walk.

Sintra is a mystical place, with castles tucked into thickly treed, hilly expanses. Palácio da Monserrate was the summer residence of the kings of Portugal, built before them by Moorish royalty. This is a place of unexpected beauty.

The train stops in the town of Canto. Narrow cobblestone lanes are decorated with brightly colored streamers that hang from streetlamps, remnants of a recent festival. It is like arriving on the page of a fairytale.

Old women fill glass jugs at a blue-tiled, Moorish fountain, so I take advantage and top up my large bottle for the walk. The water is sweet and cold, just as it was from the Italian aqueduct-fed fountains in Rome. The palace is an hour's climb, and I begin to walk to Monserrate, allegedly the most romantic sight in all of Portugal. It will suit my licentious mood.

Winding my way up the quiet, ancient road in reverie, a car approaches and slows. Men yell out what I can only assume are Portuguese catcalls. At their piercing whistles, I turn. Three young men perched out of the windows whoop and holler and make macho noises. Maneuvering the car within inches of me, one reaches out with a big smile to slap my ass. I scream out profanities in surprise. And mortification. From Venice to Capri, I escaped Italy without a single of the famed Italian pinches or slaps, and now, on a back road in Portugal, I am ambushed. Laughing, they speed off around a sharp curve. With my dignity bruised, I approach an old, majestic house and pull out my camera to take a photo, and to rest. Cooling off, a few minutes later I laugh at this little stunt.

Dillydallying my way through the magical landscape, I half expect a wizard to jump out of the trees. As I drift from one thought to the next, I wonder if Jean-François has noticed my scars.

When I was a small girl, my auntie Simone died slowly and painfully. I vividly recall the five-hour road trips to see her. The smell of the hospital spoke of decay and death. She lay in bed, weak, her skin pallid, her red hair fuzzy and splayed on the pillow. Subsequently, my father would receive emergency calls asking him to come quickly, the doctors warning that she was close to death. She was dying from breast cancer.

She was a nun who bore two children after leaving the convent for marriage and a secular life. Our secret emotional lives can bear the fruit of catastrophic destruction. After the indoctrination of a strict, masochistic order, I suspect shame and guilt played a part in the cancerous tumor that slowly and voraciously attacked her femininity and sexuality, ultimately killing her.

A child already overwhelmed by a problematic home life, the horror of seeing my aunt in this condition, solidified the belief that breast cancer was a vicious monster and unquestionably the worst thing that could ever happen to anyone.

At twenty-nine years of age, I got it.

I have always been my own harshest critic, but I love my breasts. They were (and are) lovely and give me much pleasure. Although young and in a state of shock, I had the foresight to sit with the surgeon and outline my needs and concerns. I reminded him of my age and told him to take the utmost care, both cosmetically, and in regard to nerves and sensation with the lumpectomy. In handwriting squeezed between the narrow lines, I stipulated on my consent form that under no circumstances was he to proceed with anything resembling a mastectomy. I went so far as to request that in the operating room there would be no talk of gloom.

Aside from aesthetics and pleasure, breasts represent feminine strength, and hold deep importance to me. They are an intricate part of the female body's complex meridian and energy system, and I do not believe they should be removed unnecessarily. The surgeon was brilliant and empathetic, and did as I asked. Even though I am not thrilled to have a deep gash in my armpit, and a scar on my breast, with lost fullness, it is becoming less apparent as time goes on. I am aware that many women willingly lop off their breasts at the slightest hint of cancer, but I was more afraid of the loss of my wholeness than I was of death.

Six years from my ordeal, I am still wary of my mortality. *Should I tell him? Will I scare him away?*

Still newlyweds when we got the news, my husband was frightened and unsure of what to do, what to say, what to feel.

I am not so concerned with ugliness; what I wonder is how this man may feel getting involved with a woman who could die young.

I shake myself back to the moment and my lush surroundings. The panoramic view from where I sit is spectacular, and it's obvious why English poets were enamored by this place. Around another curve, I see the little white car approaching with the three young men inside. They slow the car again and all have reproachful looks on their faces as they pull up and stop.

"We are sorry. We just have fun. Really. We so sorry. No harm?"

They are adorably Portuguese-cute, and all three smile, begging forgiveness, their hands up in mock prayer. I can't help but smile and say yes, forgiven, no harm.

Walking for hours up and down the hilly road, I lose track of time. Eventually, I snap out of my trance to realize I have found no palace. At a house on the side of the road, strangers call a taxi for a ride back to the station, shaking their heads in disbelief that I have walked this far. The town is definitely not within walking distance; I don't know if I am even on the road to Monserrate anymore.

Exhausted, I drift into a dreamy and delicious nap with the rocking of the train, headed back to a French kiss in Lisbon.

The night I met Jean-François, I told him I came to Portugal because of the festivals. He has now made it his objective to ensure that I get to experience them. I feel truly taken care of as someone of great value, maybe for the first time in my life.

Giggling our way down the streets, Jean-François carries my knapsack. I have never laughed this much with anyone, and my body hums from the effects.

Deep in the Alfama, we find a sizeable neighborhood festival. A massive barbeque is neatly lined with aromatic meats, and we squeeze into a spot amongst the cramped tables with a good vantage point for people watching. We eat charred barbequed chicken and salad between kisses.

A band plays in the square and people of all ages dance together. At the obelisk, we sit amongst the dancers. I must join in, trying to coax Jean-François.

"*Mais non!* I am a ridiculous dancer."

While I tug on his arm and plead with him, an old man takes my hand. Joy bubbles and spills. I am happy to be here in this foreign city, dancing with this weathered, smiling Portuguese man, eating chicken and drinking sweet sangria, exploring Lisboa with this Frenchman, all in a quixotic haze.

Walking through the Barrio Alto, Jean-François explains points of interest and informs me of the history of the devastating earthquake of 1755. The quake struck on the morning of All Saints' Day while most of the city was at mass. I ponder how many Lisboans faith's were tested, or lost, to have so many die while in worship. The streets are steep, so we stop to rest near a funicular railway.

We saunter our way back to his small room, but I want to run. Anticipation grows with each step; I can't wait to get to his bed. At last, we arrive on his inky, unlit street, and he fumbles at the entrance with the ancient key. Against the wall of the creaking elevator he presses into me with deep kisses.

Oh. My. God.

His hands move up and down my body, commandingly. He laughs as he picks me up, throws the door open, and places me on his bed. I am ripe fruit on cool sheets. I am his.

I have always had a predilection for men with wide shoulders, and strong chests, and have a bent for visual piquancy. Initially, I was surprised by his long, straight physique, but his manner and his being has shifted my paradigm; all of him intensely turns me on. Nuzzling into his neck, I breathe in his scent. We are hungry to explore each other, new lovers in the delectable dawn of discovery.

My senses wildly heightened, he need not do much for my pleasure. But he does. I am swept away in a crest of pheromones; my mind and body in rapture—a word I never understood before, but now do—now that I am being taken wholly, willingly.

My mind is deliriously empty. I don't know what day it is, and I don't care about tomorrow. If time exists, I cannot feel it. I have never been more in the moment than at this moment.

Arriving at my *pensão* disheveled, and a little later than normal this morning, the owner realizes I have been away all night, and gives me a disapproving grimace. I am no longer in his good graces.

I strip, tossing my clothes to the floor and fall back into bed, unused to the early mornings and late nights.

Midday, I eat a lusciously fresh Portuguese meal in the Baixa, and afterwards stretch out in a park to read. The heat is bearable in the shade, and the birds busily twitter above in the magnificent oak tree, connecting me to the pulse of the Earth.

Lisbon graces me with a slow, sensuous day, while seedlings begin to stir in the soil of my heart.

Jean-François arrives at my *pensão* this evening with a grin, excited. He has researched the *fêtes* in Lisbon, and on a side street we find the large square in the Alfama with a grand festival in full swing. The evening is humid and still sweltering hot, and women sit with fans aflutter in an attempt to cool themselves.

A stocky woman in an impeccable white suit marches across the cobblestone square with a tiny, ladylike girlfriend in tow, trying to catch my eye.

Jean-François fetches us a drink, and we situate ourselves on a set of steps, leaning on the rail to watch the activities. The white-suited woman spots me again and locks eyes on me. Catching on to her partner's interest, a mild panic washes across her girl-friend's face. Given that I am clearly here with a man, her interest is comical.

French words from my childhood pop into my head at opportune moments, surprising me. On our family visits, my French grandfather whom, to my seven-year-old eyes, looked like a wizened turtle, walked me to the cheese factory near his home.

Hand in hand, we would saunter ever so slowly, and he would mutter foreign words to me. His horrid wife, Step *grand-mère*— the Wicked Witch of Winnipeg—made the grandchildren speak only French in her presence, and I am oddly grateful to her at this moment.

Jean-François asks if I am concerned about our age difference. To my mind, age is determined by the essence and energy of a person. I have known people who are biologically thirty, yet exude the air of a person many decades older. I know my energy is younger than my thirty-five years, and this is what concerns him, but the eight years between us is as insignificant as dust in the wind.

The castle looms over this ancient section of the city, making the evening more dream-like. The cultural blend and integration of the inhabitants creates an exotic atmosphere. With Brazilian, Latin, and African influences from the former Portuguese colonies, I am moved by the cadence and archaic soul of the music. My body involuntarily sways to each new rhythm, and I close my eyes to breathe in the antiquity of my surroundings.

White Suit has been attempting to get my attention, and decides to make her grand gesture. A *Fado* is now playing, and she begins to dance with sweeping movements as dramatic as the mournful strains of the song. A handsome woman, and rather self-possessed, she watches me to make sure I am watching her.

Emboldened, she dances near us, all the while fixed on me, confusing her skittish girlfriend. Jean-François at last notices her efforts, and looks at me with eyebrows cocked. He is amused, but confounded about what she thinks she will achieve with this attempted seduction.

As the fiesta winds down, we leave, hands intertwined, relishing the quietude that has enveloped the Alfama. I am glad I have brought all of my pretty dresses. I feel free—liberated to be myself completely, to let my feminine persona run wild. The masculine self of my workaday life has vanished like an unwanted ghost in the midnight mist that has appeared on these steep streets.

How is it that, with a stranger, we can find instant intimacy and ease, yet with another it can be months, or even years, and we do not ever attain it, forever a mild trace of inhibition or awkwardness lurking in the shadows? Somewhere, there must be an explanation in the quantum physics of life's matrix. Possibly it is the weaving of lifetimes together. Have I known him intimately in another time? I prefer to think we don't have to come back to this heavily and harshly lessoned planet, but I have seen too much evidence to the contrary.

We kiss and touch as though we have known each other for infinity. A sense of warm comfort and easy familiarity exists between us. Inside me, a voice that was hanging in a void says, *finally, I have found you. I knew you were here amongst these strangers.*

Like a woman on an Arthurian quest, I feel that I have found my Grail.

It is the weekend and we have plans for our first beach day together. I sit on Jean-François' lap as we wait for the train, feeling both rebellious and emancipated to be able to do so without a trace of disapproval from anyone here. I am caught up in the amorousness of the city and, when in Lisbon, I am tickled to do as the Lisboans do.

I ask Jean-François about France. His culture is far more demonstrative than mine, but I am curious to know if the public displays of affection are as overt and plentiful as here, especially what I observe in the parks.

"*Non*," he says, "definitely we kiss and embrace everywhere, but it is even more prevalent here."

We concur that we are lucky to meet here. Having caught Lisbon's libidinous bug, I am now conscious of how stifled I am by my own culture, and how much I adore touch, anywhere.

It is a challenge to find even a tiny square of sand on the crowded beach, but eventually we squeeze in between two families. Jean-François refuses sunscreen, unconcerned that he is already lightly sunburned. I, on the other hand, ask him to slather my white skin in lotion. Lingering over each inch of bare skin, he massages the warm cream into my body. The sun and the sand are already an aphrodisiac; this sensuous contact nudges me into a bliss-soaked state.

After a period of contented silence, I sit up to take in the scene. Everyone in Lisbon must be out today enjoying the weather. Previously, while investigating the city, I have noticed the loveliness of the Lisboan girls but, here on the beach, as I watch these nubile beauties stride by with long, brown legs and ripe, full breasts, I begin to feel intimidated. I am an average Canadian woman. I now have scars on my body, and have always had a small 'Boyton belly' (my mother's side), no matter my weight. I have yearned for pin-like arms and an hourglass waistline.

The European lifestyle of walking everywhere, especially up all of these mountainous streets, keeps these women in shape in a natural way that puts to shame the artificiality of the gym-obsessed with their desperate, hungry look. There are no hard lines to these women's bodies, only a curvy smoothness that is at once firm and soft. Brushing sand off my conspicuously white legs, I wonder why this romantic, attractive Frenchman has chosen me over this profusion of luscious Latina-ness.

Suddenly, he takes my face in his hands.

"*Non!*" he pronounces.

"What?" I ask, startled.

"Don't think such thoughts. These girls have nothing of interest to me. You are a beautiful woman, and I want *you*."

I am shocked by my transparency, but his determined kiss dissolves my doubt. Relaxing into the safe shelter of his growing devotion, I float in and out of a sun induced-slumber.

A French couple with a young child is seated next to us at a popular, old world restaurant in *el centro* tonight. As is the norm here, the tables are in tight proximity. Jean-François greets them with a smile. Later, the fidgety little girl gets up to play, bored with the confinement.

"*Mon Dieu!* She is so pretty," Jean-François says as he places a hand under her chin. I freeze. Grasping both of her small hands in his, he affectionately talks to her. His face reveals sincerity and a love of children. She lights up with the focus of his attention. It is moving to watch, but I tensely await the parents' response, expecting them to pull her away from him any moment. Studying their faces, my shoulders release in relief; they are beaming with pride.

Ah, yes ... I have forgotten—I am in Europe, where people still touch and do not live in a perpetual state of suspicion that every stranger is a pervert seeking to harm their children. It is a moment of human contact at its finest, and I am disheartened to realize that I live in a place where this type of caring encounter is now extinct. How it must sadden kind old men.

Our meals arrive and Jean-François' tenderness is now directed toward me. He feeds me savory bites of grilled fish and herbed potatoes. Everything in this country tastes just picked or freshly caught. The food is simple, yet divine. We sip local wine and he entertains me with funny stories, while I search my pocket dictionary for words that elude me. Like the little girl, I feel myself glow under his undivided attention.

Attempting discretion, two women on the other side of our table have been keenly observing us since they arrived. Anonymity allows me to act as I wish, and I wish to act like a love-struck teenager, in spite of their watchful eyes.

They get up to leave and, unable to resist, they walk over to me.

"Excuse us, but we have to ask ... *wherever* did you find him?"

I laugh loudly.

Jean-François looks confused, and I attempt a poor translation. They tell me they are Air Canada flight attendants on a three-day visit to Lisbon. They say they have been observing us and are fascinated; they feel like they have been watching a fabulous romance movie. Once they realize he doesn't understand them, they gush on.

"He's so charming. My God."

"And handsome! We'd love to find such a man in our travels. And he's clearly smitten with you."

They leave, telling me I am a very lucky girl.

And I am.

High waves crash the coastline on this windy day. Jean-François has rented a car to take me on a daytrip. His impeccable periwinkle shirt draws the blue out of his eyes today. While he drives, I run my fingers through his hair. I am entranced by the thick waves and salt and pepper richness of it. He speaks, and I kiss his cheek. I graze gentle kisses across his ear and down his neck.

"*Mon Dieu,*" he groans, pulling the car onto a small side road.

Placing a hand under my chin, he kisses me. We embrace tightly for a long while.

"*Je t'aime*," he whispers.

My heart skips ten thousand beats.

My head swirls as we drive off toward the small town he has chosen to go to. He has just told me he loves me. I know it's as mad as a March hare. The swiftness of us is surreal, yet as real as anything.

With an equal penchant for play, we sneak into yards to admire gardens, and sip lattes on street patio cafés. We splash at the ocean's edge and pick shells. It seems like a long time since I had a partner in crime.

Somewhat exhausted by the constant translating in my mind—it takes serious concentration to communicate, but it is an adventure—I delight in the feel of a foreign language on my lips, and the creation of new pathways in my brain. I thrive on learning. This is the language of my ancestors, and I feel a much deeper affinity for my French roots than for my British.

Also, this man has an intensity that burns brightly and requires alertness and energy. Born under the sign of the lion, he has the presence of the king of the jungle. He is self-assured and has many clear-cut opinions about all aspects of life, from the choice of a small, inexpensive gift, to the Revolution's impact on French culture. His mind is analytical and logical—an engineer's mind. He appears perplexed by my cryptic creativity and esoteric ideas.

I have two distinct sides: the type A, perfectionist, business persona built through years of indoctrination out of necessity; and then the artistic, nomadic, wild woman. On my sojourns, I allow my gypsy girl to take over and run free. She is my truest self; the one who longs to escape forever, free from the confines of societal indoctrination, and the rules of the corporati. With the heart of a wanderer, she is too outrageous for her motherland. Secretly,

I call her Jacqueline, the name that I learned my mother had chosen for me, the one derailed by my father due to its 'Frenchness'—apparently not a good thing in the year I was born.

Even with my plentiful energy and perpetual curiosity, this man is igniting dormant places and awakening unused parts of my psyche. My body is becoming an untamed tropical garden, teeming with fragrant flowers that are unfurling with dizzying rapidity, lush with ripe fruit dripping sweetness, undulating like the velveteen wings of a hundred thousand monarchs.

River of Gold

Once you have traveled, the voyage never ends, but is played out over and over again in the quietest chambers. The mind can never break off from the journey.
—Pat Conroy

SAFELY TUCKED INTO MY SEAT BY JEAN-FRANÇOIS, I SIT ON the bus to Oporto. He has insisted that I keep my plans to go north to see the land of port wine; he doesn't want to be the reason I miss out on experiencing what I came so far to see. The bus makes its way to my destination and I am enamored by the countryside. At a stop in Fátima I expect something monumental, because of the famed apparitions of the Virgin Mary and the number of pilgrims who have come here, but it appears to be an ordinary little town.

I arrive in the early afternoon with a breathtaking entrance to the city of Oporto. It is built on the gorge of the Douro River (River of Gold), which winds its way to the Spanish border. Four massive bridges flank the river—two are designed by Eiffel, the metalwork clearly reminiscent of the Parisian Eiffel Tower. The working class character of this city feels completely different than the old world grandeur of Lisbon.

I easily find a room in a hotel by the name of Residencial de Paris. How apropos. I walk the streets of the business core of Oporto, and then return to shower and change for dinner.

Allegedly, the workmen's bars have the best meals for a good value. On a winding street, I spot a window full of tasty looking *piri-piri* chickens roasting on spits in one of the bars.

A sea of heads turn as I enter, and all conversation stops in this full-to-capacity pub. There is not a woman to be found, but I refuse to turn around and leave. Self-consciously, I make my way to the single open space at the counter. Once seated, conversations resume, and the smirking bartender asks what I will have to drink. Two curious men next to me ask where I am from, nod approvingly (I suspect this is the extent of their English), then go back to their daily banter. The inexpensive wine is of surprisingly good quality, but then again, I am in wine country where even lowly table vino is said to be superior. Fussing over me, the bartender delivers my platter of food with a flourish. As promised, the hearty man-sized meal is excellent. While I sip and savor the heavy red wine, I write Jean-François a postcard. It will arrive after I do, but I want to send it anyway.

I feel every bit a woman again. My husband and I had an intense chemistry and, with our mutual interests and compatible character traits, I felt fortunate to have married a man for whom I felt such magnetism. When he began to refuse my advances for a month at a time, alarms sounded. With his drive, I was fiercely confused. I began to have nightmares of infidelity, and would awaken angry. When I told him of my bad dreams, he would breezily brush away my fears. But my gnawing instincts would not let me fall into a secure slumber.

Months after our separation, I pressed for the truth. I needed to know if my intuition was to be trusted, or if I had built up a story from an overactive or paranoid imagination.

A 'deny until you die' type of man, it took some convincing to extract an honest answer from him. Eventually, he confessed to cheating. With no valid excuse to stray (if ever there is one), I was stricken with a stabbing sense of betrayal. Not once had I spurned his advances. But the insidiousness of alcohol in a man's body and brain needs no reason.

Three years ago, when my husband left our home for the last time, not only was I afflicted with hysterical paralysis, I could not breathe for the grief. I did not think I would survive the dense quagmire of my sadness. Tonight, as my body tingles with happiness, that angst is a distant memory.

Meandering after dinner, I ask a man to take my picture in the main square. He in turn invites me out for the evening and I decline, far too deeply infatuated with my French lover to allow my senses to be sullied by another man.

The buzz of Oporto awakens me, and I make my way to the train station for Barcelos after dawdling over breakfast. My guidebook tells me this is the home of the oldest and largest outdoor market in Europe. Probably at the end of an early morning shift, the ticket seller is dozing in his booth. He informs me that the market closes at noon, the train's ETA, but I go anyway.

The ride itself is poetry. With verdant rolling hills, each knoll of the countryside fills the travel cache in my mind. Barcelos is even further nestled into the north of Portugal, and its days-gone-by charm is worth the trip. At the market, I discover that today, for some unbeknownst reason, it will remain open until sunset. Serendipity is on my side.

Overwhelmed with scents and sights, it is as massive as stated. Endless rows of dazzling flower bouquets dizzy the senses with their scent, and bedraggled women in dark dresses and headscarves stand, selling their wares, their apron pockets heavy with coins.

Sausages of every shape and size hang from stalls, and the intestines of various animals are roped around booths in great bunches to dry in the sun. Winding through the labyrinth, I leave the unpleasant smell of raw meat, and walk into the sweet, yeasty aroma of freshly baked bread.

Gossiping women sit on the ground, absent-mindedly fluffing and preening their chickens to entice customers. Watching these contented birds being stroked, as beloved pets would be, I feel queasy. Little do they know their fate. A box of rabbits sit with noses twitching, also unaware. I consider grabbing the container to rescue the creatures, wondering what the consequence would be if I were to set them free in the nearby field. I am not a vegetarian, but I have seduced myself into thinking the skinless, boneless chicken breasts I buy in tidy packages don't actually come from cute little animals.

A lone woman in a black headscarf dozes in the noonday heat, surrounded by heaps of vegetables and fruits piled high on the ground. Coming to the end of the row, I find a heavy old woman resting on her knees and leaning on her elbows (not a sight you see every day in Canada), appearing to be intently counting a mountain of beans.

Near the market, a restaurant has come highly recommended, and I have my sights set on it for lunch. Traipsing in a circle outside the periphery of the Feira de Barcelos, I am unable to find it. A tired wooden bench beckons, so I sit down to regroup. Having made it this far, I cannot give up. The quest for good food is an important part of any journey I take, even if to a small Saskatchewan town on a business trip in my sales life.

On my second attempt around, I spot it. I am seated in the center of the large, bustling restaurant, and my waiter warmly introduces himself. An eclectic mix of sharply dressed white-collar business people, sturdy blue-collar workers, and the old women from the stalls of the market surround me.

An impressive wood-fire oven in the open kitchen has a baker hovering nearby, carefully overseeing his goods. I order, and the waiter presents my half bottle of *vinho verde* with pride. It is one of their finest local wines, and I am soon to discover it is not available anywhere else in Portugal, or the world, for that matter. A chilled red, which I've never had before, it is one of the most delicious I have ever tasted. I swirl it around my mouth, and it is so full-bodied I can almost chew it.

The waiter returns with a dish of assorted olives, and two small rounds of cheese, accompanied by a hot loaf of bread. Compliments of the house, he tells me in Portuguese, but this much I now understand. I have chosen a traditional pork dish, so I remind myself to eat these delectable morsels sparingly. *Good luck*. The out-of-this-world bread is a coarse, natural, peasant style, served with freshly churned butter. I allow myself to groan a food orgasm; nobody can hear me in the din anyway. The cheeses are farm fresh, and unlike any I know of. Even the olives, which I normally don't care for, are earthy, salty, and delicious. The salad arrives on a large metal platter. It is just a simple mix of greens and tomatoes with olive oil and lemon, but tastes as though freshly picked from the back garden of the restaurant. Maybe it has been.

I observe the crowd, particularly fascinated with the old women. In spite of the heat, they wear thick, black stockings, and dark *babushkas* cover their hair. Many are mustached, and all have large, heavily calloused hands with dirt embedded under their fingernails. These are serious workwomen, stocky and sturdy, still living the old life of an old world. I am taken with the concept that their ways are still alive and well—we have not infiltrated the lives of these people. Crossing time, I have entered another era where life exists without the bombardment of the Information Age. We work our way into pristine corners of the world, with our fast-paced lives and our technology, insistent on forcing our behaviors onto people of another ilk. I silently cheer their old ways. These dissimilarities make the world rich and diverse. I pray globalization doesn't destroy it all.

When the main course arrives, I laugh aloud.

"This can't be my meal."

"*Si,*" says my waiter.

"This is for one person?"

"*Si, si!*"

In front of me sits a large oval platter with two huge pieces of grilled pork surrounded by oodles of fresh vegetables and roasted baby potatoes. I look around for someone to share this with—I can't waste this feast. An old peasant woman sits nearby with her young grandson, and I am about to ask them if they would like some of my meal, but scanning their table, I note they have double the food that I do.

With the first bite, my eyes roll back, and the waiter is amused by my pleasure. After I finish, he brings a gift with my bill. He presents me with the Barcelos rooster and gives me a small piece of paper, which explains, in English, the famous legend of the rooster's miraculous intervention to save an innocent man falsely accused of a crime. The bill for this massive feast is inconceivably low. This meal will be legendary in my personal history.

Awakened early by sparks of excitement and thoughts of Jean-François, I rise to explore the ghettos carved into the gorge. Lines of laundry billow across the buildings, children play soccer, old men chat in front of *mercados*, and women loudly gossip out windows with each other. Climbing my way up and down the streets, I see poverty, but no threat. Only benign activity with a blend of old and new.

Docked along the boardwalk on the Douro, old wooden ships bob, heavily laden with wine-filled oak barrels. Taking the walking bridge to Vila Nova de Gaia, I am at the home of the port houses and wine lodges. The boats sail down the river from the northern vineyards, a rustic and romantic sight to see.

At a patio bar, sipping sweet, thick wine in the afternoon sun, I stretch out to soak up the sights. I etch the gorge, the antiquated ships with their sails, and the sounds of the children into my mind.

I finally understand Rumi. I have time-traveled into the past where people were encouraged to run around drunkenly stupid from love's effects, in the days of poets and rogues. A fugitive from reality, it suits me well. I was born for this; it is my true nature to be this free and joy-filled. The port, winding its way through my veins and warming me, entices me to slowly re-live sweet snippets with Jean-François. Bringing him to my senses, my body purrs as though he is right here, kissing me. This hazy reminiscence makes my head swim, rousing impatience for our rendezvous tonight.

I am in love. It is illogical, but when was love ever logical? I can't think ahead of today. He is irresistible, and I have the notion that I would climb mountains to be with him.

I am booked on the 4:00 p.m. bus. I have checked out of my *pensão* in Lisbon and my Frenchman has invited me to stay with him for the balance of my trip.

I leave Oporto, happy to have been, but excited to go.

Jean-François stands, awaiting my bus at the station, with an expectant smile. He ravishes without a touch, and a rush tingles through me, down to my toes. Never have I met a man who is so frequently excited with such little provocation, and everywhere we go we must stop along our way to wait. Right now, we sit chortling while he cools off. The knowledge that a look or a brief kiss can incite him stirs and strengthens my sense of femininity. I too am in a perpetual flux of excitement.

He has chosen a lovely little café for dinner tonight. Giddily, we eat and talk. I share my perceptions of Oporto, and tell him of my poetic adventure up to Barcelos, all the while using my dictionary. I am beginning to remember words and phrases, and ask for help with proper pronunciation. Jean-François is intimidated, and embarrasses easily when he attempts English, but I have no inhibitions about learning languages. He chooses not to speak much English, compelling me to learn more French. It is a goal I've had for a long time, so, for me, it's like a romantic immersion course.

Watching families play games and dogs chase balls in a park, walking hand in hand with this man, I am gloriously gratified.

On our way back to his room, Jean-François pulls me under a majestic old tree on the *avenida*, my back pressed against the trunk as he kisses me. We remain there until the darkness settles, the slow kisses rendering me deliciously dizzy. Dormancy begets more dormancy. I have been lured out of a closed-bud season, and have entered a salubrious spring.

The humid, San Francisco-style, vintage railcar is crowded and noisy en route to Belém. A young man nuzzles in close behind me in the standing-room-only car, but I let his bravado pass without visible reaction; I am too content to cause a scene.

Scanning the street signs, I jump off at the famed bakery. It is warm with the scent of bread and sugar. The pastries are every bit as wonderful as promised. I lick freshly whipped cream off my fingers and brush the powdery icing sugar from my face and blouse.

Walking toward the nearby fan of fountains, a man sitting on a park bench with a glazed look catches my eye. As I get closer, I notice his pants are undone. I take a sharp turn across the grass as far away as possible. Overheated, I pick up a coin—a lucky *escudo*—from the cement bench, slip it in my purse, and lie down under the light mist to cool off.

Eyes closed, the impressions of the Manueline architecture, and the everyday life of Belém pass through my mind. Just walking through the streets of a European city is an event. I adore this continent. It is so vastly different from my young country.

I think about what has transpired since I arrived. Jean-François generously takes me out each night to a new café or festival. He knows the city intimately and shares his haunts with me. Lisbon bustles and is alive with activity. The culture, the gastronomic pleasures, and the hum of this city stimulate my sense and sensibility. Life for a girl like me doesn't get any better than unfettered days investigating a foreign country with oneself, and then evenings in the company of a sexy, funny Frenchman, followed by long nights of *amour extraordinaire*.

Roaming through Italy solo, I felt at home in a way I couldn't have expected. Returning to Canada was like being dropped into a black and white, one-dimensional movie. I can only imagine what it will feel like, going back after this exhilarating interlude in Lisbon.

Refreshed, I shake off thoughts of my life back home to further investigate the wonders of this city.

Estoril is a pretty place. The bartender at the quaint beach bar looks like a young, Portuguese Antonio Banderas. *Mamma mia*, he is beautiful. He skillfully prepares a tall *caipirinha* and places it in front of me with a smile. The fresh mint and sweet lime are revitalizing.

"Where you are coming from?" he asks.

After a brief conversation about Canada, he wanders off to choose new music, clearly finding the English a struggle. With the light bongo roll of *Falling Into You*, the title song of my favorite album this year, I turn with a start. It always seems incongruous, yet comforting, to hear the familiarity of your own music in another country. Singing along under my breath, I peruse a magazine. The bartender cleans his small café, and then sits to read a book. It is just he and I here on this weekday afternoon, and I enjoy his quiet company and gentle aura.

My mind is full of Jean-François.

"*I see us, inside of each other ...*" Celine croons.

It is not that I believe him to be perfect; he is as flawed as any other human. I catch glimpses of an almost aristocratic air of superiority, and I haven't missed his failings. Having had other foreign flings, I am no stranger to the thrill. Strongly attracted to the exoticness of non-waspy men, I thrive on the fun of being shown a new place with someone exciting. I fly off, satiated, never to return—*adios* and *arrivederci*.

In Lisbon with this Frenchman, I do not feel the same. I am swept away in my response to him. I feel safe for the first time ever, taken care of in a way that I feel a woman should be. And I am beginning to believe that I have been mistaken; love is not a landmine—it is a benevolent place of goodness and beauty.

All of the tightness of my everyday life has dissolved. I am lightness and fluidity. The tension that pervades my body at home, that which I was unaware of, is now gone. I am unfamiliarly untethered; I am a me I have not previously known.

A poignant description of love comes to my mind, one I heard in a movie. When you fall in love and someone falls in love with you, you see yourself through their eyes. They love you and adore you and, in turn, you fall in love with yourself. In the movie, the lead character told his wife he had fallen in love with another woman, fourteen years into their marriage, because he needed to remember all that was good about himself. After so many years, even within a loving marriage, he claimed he couldn't find that feeling without the feedback of another. It was an apt description of what makes falling in love so heady, and I know I am falling in love with myself for the first time in my life.

Deep in conversation at the bank machine, a bundle of *escudos* disappear, siphoned back into the machine before Jean-François can grab it. $300 worth of Portuguese cash has vanished into the wall of this foreign bank. We laugh in amazement at the audacity of this system, far too quickly reclaiming his withdrawal. He says he will go to the bank at lunchtime this week to retrieve his money.

One of Jean-François' colleagues has highly recommended a restaurant situated on the hill that snakes up to Castle São Jorge. We titter over one thing or another on our climb up the slope, and are out of breath when we arrive at the charming café. The private table on the patio overlooking the city reminds me of a scene in *Roman Holiday*.

Jean-François tells me about the scolding he received from his landlady this morning. My postcard arrived from Oporto and she had, naturally, intercepted it. She wanted to know, in no uncertain terms, why he was receiving a romantic note from another woman while in the throes of a new relationship with me.

"She is a lovely girl, and so *gentil*. What is the matter with you?" she berated him. It apparently took some convincing to get her to believe that the postcard was, in fact, from me.

I don't know if it is my French DNA, my Sagittarian predilection for the foreign, or just the pure loveliness of the language, but I am punch-drunk when Jean-François speaks. This man looks so deeply into my eyes, it is as though he is searching to know everything, each fragment of me. He listens intently, and if he doesn't understand, he seeks clarification—nothing is glossed over.

What would Lisbon look like without him? The world appears fresh and new with these love-tinted lenses. Everything is more vivid, sharper, and awash in pulsating color. Would the food taste as good? Would this place look as mystical? I can't say. Everything he does seduces me and, each time we make love, I find myself falling deeper into watery depths that I have no desire to leave, even if I may risk drowning.

I am back at 'Antonio's' bar in Estoril for a light breakfast. He has one of my songs on repeat; he is broody and clearly in love with someone, and we commiserate.

After the strongest noonday sunrays have passed, I move to a comfortable spot on the beach and read *One Room in a Castle*, the perfect travel story for this adventure. Two men sit close by and strike up a conversation. They are Swiss: one with stunning looks, the other not quite as Euro-handsome, but charming. Offering to buy me a drink, they regale me with stories about life in Switzerland, and the many things they have been doing in Portugal.

Realizing we're all ravenous, they invite me to a late lunch at a nearby beach café. We spend the afternoon together, sipping cocktails and getting silly, laughing ourselves senseless as we test the latest invention, the self-cleaning pay toilets on the street corner. They ask me out for the evening and spend an hour trying to convince me to go, even though I explain that I am staying with a Frenchman I have met here.

"So what? You don't owe him anything."

I know they are right—I am not tied to him—but at this point, I would be wounded if he chose to spend a night on the town with other women while I was in Lisbon.

I catch the train and try to sober up in a cool shower back at the room. Jean-François returns from work, and gesticulates wildly as he tells me about the scene in the bank today. The manager pleaded innocence to the bank machine's *escudo* abduction until Jean-François threatened to create an uproar in the crowded lunchtime lines. The money was returned.

He asks about my day, and is not at all impressed that the Swiss have entertained me the entire day. I am unused to the jealous nature of his European personality; it is an unacceptable trait in my culture and, even if we feel it, we have learned to pretend not to. I am crazy about the feeling of being with him, but one fact he doesn't yet know: he may capture my heart, he may bewitch my body, but he will never possess and tame the untamable.

At a minuscule bar in the center of the park-like boulevard of Avenida da Liberdade soccer games play incessantly on the television, the air thick with smoke, the men either cheering or cursing. I pass it each day and their enthusiasm has become infectious. Poking my head inside, I ask how Portugal is faring, even though I have no knowledge of European football.

After lunch, I lay on a tree-shaded bench in a square, and daydream about the den of spies swarming wartime Lisbon. Where did they meet? Right here in this park? In my spy-novel phase, I dreamed of visiting pre-Glasnost Russia, fantasizing that I'd roam the streets of Moscow, acting suspiciously, to see if the KGB would trail me. In Trafalgar Square in London, I watched for Ludlum-esque spies. Only in my imagination am I courageous enough for a life of espionage.

Locating a payphone just off the busy Art Nouveau section where I will shop today for gifts and mementos, I make a call home. I have promised to touch base at least twice, to let everyone know I am alive. My friend Donna has asked that I dedicate one of my calls to her, and I am certain that she will appreciate my story. Entertaining her with my romantic escapade in Lisbon, my excitement is contagious; she squeals and asks a barrage of questions. I also tell her to pass along this message to my family: If I die on this trip, I leave Earth a wildly happy woman.

And I mean it with all of my being.

Chivalry is not dead yet. Not here. Our culture, our liberation, should not have gone so far as to destroy the male-female equipoise that existed for millennia. All human beings are *unequivocally* equal: men and women, black, yellow and white, laborer and white-collar worker. But what does that have to do with men expressing their innate nature, and women theirs? Men helping women, opening doors, a man's hand on one's back meant as an act of protection—the natural order of things—has been disrupted and left women like me adrift in a sea of confusion, with an overly developed sense of independence concealing a constant craving for rapport. Where is the happy medium?

I love my strength, but I want to soften. I don't want to do it all myself. I want strong arms to comfort me, especially after the discombobulating awfulness of the C-word.

Jean-François and I have slept in, rolled up in the sheets of the old brass bed in his tiny room. It is the weekend and we eat at the *pâtisserie*, lingering over a double order of cappuccinos. We meander, spending a lazy Sunday afternoon at a nearby park. Children play and old men debate and we are content to sit and observe the sweet essence of the culture.

Hypnotically, he caresses my hair while I lay on the tree-shaded bench, my head in his lap. Oxytocin, the exquisite hormone that bonds people together, pulses through my body.

Describing his country home outside of a small town, Jean-François recites the ingredients of his favorite Sunday dinner in detail, and the things he buys fresh from the surrounding village markets. A man who enjoys cooking, he says would very much like to make a feast for me. I close my eyes and visualize him cooking for me in a large kitchen in an antiquated stone farmhouse in the south of France.

He speaks of his son with affection, and describes French life in vibrant prose. I can smell the sun-kissed lavender fields, touch the warm back of the white stallion, see the peeling paint on the dilapidated barn by the house. I can feel the crackling heat of a mid-summer's day, and taste his favorite Sunday meal.

He is rich with flavor, like a thick bouillabaisse, filled with deep nuances and savory spices—the antonym of the average, bland North American.

Beautiful country.

    Beautiful weather.

    Beautiful love.

Lisbon is this girl's happiness trifecta.

Since I have returned from Oporto, Jean-François and I have passed every spare minute together. We rest on old, wooden chairs at a beach patio café and, soon afterwards, he leaves to find a battery for his camera. A friendly black man approaches me to sell trinkets, and we begin a conversation. He has happy, crinkly eyes, and I enjoy answering his questions. Dressed in brightly colored traditional African clothing, he tells me fascinating things about his homeland.

Upon returning, Jean-François gives the man a disapproving look. The seller scoots away, and Jean-François begins to lecture me about speaking with men like this. I am annoyed at the insinuation that I do not have good instincts, and bothered that his words are tinged with bigotry. We begin to argue as we walk down the beach, but we must use my dictionary for this disagreement, angrily passing it to one another in an effort to find the right word or two. Eventually the ridiculousness of this exchange strikes me, and I begin to laugh. His harshness melts away, and he too laughs. Argument over.

We take in touristic sights, walking for hours in the heat of midday. One thing I can say for certain: I did not know I could laugh and play like this. Everything seems ridiculously funny and, at times, I massage my cheeks because they hurt. The mirth is a tonic that courses through every fiber of my body, making me feel strong and energetic.

There is tremendous relief in the letting go, in succumbing, in dropping the shield of resistance. I am malleable—softer and more vulnerable than I have ever known myself to be.

I have stepped into a movie. We are Hepburn and Tracy. We are Bogie and Bacall. I am Lady Chatterley, and he is my Mellors.

Today marks three days to my departure. Jean-François and I savor each other's company, but we have both become quiet and pensive. Alluding to it before, he asks me to stay. He will be leaving shortly for France, and has a holiday planned with his son along the French Riviera. He wants me to change my ticket and go home with him. The idea is insane, but tempting.

I do not want to leave this man.

We have returned to the Baixa for a melancholic late evening glass of wine at the outdoor bar where we first locked eyes, under the same yellow umbrella I sat beneath writing postcards. Discussing our feelings, we have no idea how to resolve the dilemma we find ourselves faced with.

It is absurd. He lives in France and I live in Canada, worlds apart. We have only known each other for three weeks, yet each day our feelings grow exponentially, like Jack's beanstalk. How can we feel this way so soon? How many thousands of lovers in how many places have faced a similar predicament?

In spite of my inner Bohemian, I am a commonsensical woman. I have a secure job with the best boss in the world. I have a nice home to return to—my sanctuary. I have a loving family, a strong network, and a sisterhood of friends whom I love beyond measure.

My European escape plot propagated and spread through my fantasies after my dream vacation in Italy last year. But the idea was squashed by rationale. What would I do there? What would I say to my family and friends? Why give up the security (whatever that really means) of my life? As much as the idea of running off to France appeals to me, I have a full and rich life to return to.

Reluctantly, I decline his offer, but it doesn't quell the inextricable spell this man has cast over me.

Almost skipping, I am on my way to an appointment at a chic salon on Avenida da Liberdade to have my hair straightened and blown out for my last night out with Jean-François. Unruly in the humidity, I want one good hair day before I leave. It is with difficulty that I explain what I want done, but the stylists pick up the electricity swirling around me, and excitedly create.

They convince me to have my nails and feet done pretty in pink, while I peruse Portuguese magazines. I get back to the room before Jean-François does, to be ready when he arrives, presenting myself like a rose-colored blossom.

We have agreed that, for tonight, we will set aside our angst over our parting tomorrow—we will fully embrace our last evening together in the splendor of Lisbon.

After a slow dinner, we hike to the castle. Determined to make our way there on this final night, we arrive, and are ever so enchanted. A full blue moon hangs over the Tagus, its glow shimmering and rippling on the water.

Walking along the path around the ancient walls, Jean-François grabs me from behind with a bite on my neck, laughing.

His lips work their way up into my hair, and I liquefy. Spinning me around to kiss me deeply, both hands on my face, my breath catches, erratic and shallow. This man knows how to kiss a woman. Gently, he nudges me toward a cluster of trees, both giggling in undertones in the small cove behind the bushes.

"*Je t'aime,*" he says, sotto voce.

"*Moi aussi,*" I whisper back.

Spellbound by the allure of the ancient castle, French words drift between us in the dark. Teasing with kisses along the line of my neck, he takes a handful of hair into his hands. My head whirls like a crazed eddy and I tremble, tumbling inside a hormonal orb, a rebellious runaway from the mundane.

We can no longer stop, and neither of us wants to. In this amorous city, we know that no one will complain if we are caught. Under the hex of a Lisboan moon, he takes me against the hot castle stones and, as he does so, I know nothing will ever be the same again.

Dawn is breaking as we awaken and make bittersweet love. He is mellow and subdued and looks at me with a multitude of unspoken words and a plea in his eyes; he wants me to stay. Both of us are ever so tenuous, our nerves knotted with the knowledge that I am flying off, uncertain if we will ever see each other again.

With a cup of tea in hand, one that the landlady has dropped off, I sit on the edge of the tub and watch him shave, and then pack the last of my things. He sullenly moves my cases to the door.

Idling over a European breakfast at the café around the corner, I spoon the thick froth off the cappuccino, clinging to the moment. Seated close to each other at the bar, he holds my hand and licks a drop of foam off my lips, kissing me with a light bite.

Sweet Jesus.

I do not want to go. I do not want to leave this piece of paradise—my recompense after the hell of cancer and divorce.

In the taxi, he asks what I have planned when I get home. We struggle to make small talk about my Canadian life and my job, chatter that is interrupted with the squeezing of hands and mournful kisses.

After check-in, we loiter at a bench outside of security. The inevitable is close at hand. As the boarding call bleats, I can no longer put off our farewell, and I rise to say good-bye. We stand in the longest embrace of my life. Gazing at each other, tears spill down flushed cheeks. Ever so gently, he cradles my face in his hands.

"*Je t'aime*," he says. "I miss you already. I send you off with many kisses and hugs."

"*Je t'aime*," I echo quietly.

Our hands fiercely linked, we tear away from each other, not wanting to let go with the final warning call. He kisses me deeply one last time, and I turn to leave. Walking through the gate to the large detector, I do not understand the muffled garble of the security man as I place my bags on the conveyor belt. Even as I make the motions, my body is tugging at me, aching to turn around and run to him. I look back; he stands longingly, his face ashen in spite of his tan.

What if I stayed?

What if I grabbed these bags and went to France with him?

What would happen?

My mind races as I seriously consider turning back, but my left-brain steps in and admonishes.

You have a life.

You have a career.

You have people.

My gypsy girl snaps into an ever so slightly sensible state, all the while tears streaming down my face. Sulking, I walk the long hall, and onto a jet plane that carries me far, far away from him.

TWO
CANADA

Truly. Deeply. Madly.

July

So, I love you because the entire Universe conspired to help me find you.
—Paulo Coelho, *The Alchemist*

I ARRIVE HOME TO A WARM, WELCOMING SUMMER. THE Russian elm in the backyard has burst prolifically with leafy buds, and the violet irises are in bloom. The world has swiftly transitioned to a jammy-rich color, one that I was unaware of before. From my love-hued point of view, life feels full of anticipation and brilliance. Finding a French love letter on my fax machine, I am giddy. I try to decipher it, but must take it to a friend for translation.

> *Ma Chère Wanda,*
>
> *Since our separation, I have thought a lot and, the more I think of you and us, the more I am convinced I must come to your country and see you. The three weeks with you were the most wonderful of my life. I will not forget them. Never have I known such simple beauty, in such a short time. I will pursue all of the opportunities in this world for our union.*
>
> *But if Canada is impossible for me, France will always be possible for you. I will open all the necessary doors—I promise you. My goal now is to organize a trip that will not disrupt your work too much.*

Know that I belong to you, body and soul, not like a slave, but like a partner, attentive and caring of a woman who captured me in such short time. I will not disappoint you, Wanda. It feels so good in your arms.

I adore you.

I kiss you deeply.

I love you.

JF

I am ever so pleased to see that this is not an unrequited, crazy-in-love situation.

Trying to get back to the business at hand of my workaday life, I find myself ridiculously ungrounded. Electricity eddies around me, on numerous coffee dates, when I story-tell with friends about Jean-François and my adventures in Portugal. Stunned when she first saw me après vacation, my soul sister, Lynnette, tells me I was a vision in white and full of light. She says my love is contagious, and I cannot stop smiling. I notice the infectiousness of it when I walk down a street or into a café.

A bundle of energy about to erupt, I visit clients and recite the features and benefits of new products we are currently flogging, but my mind is not on my work. A long road trip to my northern territory gives me time to hazily fantasize, and keeps me entertained while I drive the endlessly forested highways.

Jean-François has begun to phone daily. Precisely to the minute, he calls when he says he will, no matter where in Europe he is located, no matter which hotel I stay at while traveling for work. Harder than attempting French in person, the conversations are a challenge, and force me to learn the language more quickly. Frequent love letters arrive via fax, and pretty postcards and handwritten letters with dried flowers from the French countryside have begun to fill my mailbox.

This is the kind of love that motivates and inspires—love that makes you a better person. I am cleaning out drawers, and tidying closets, and getting things done that I have procrastinated over for years. Something I've long contemplated, I finally signed up for watercolor classes with a flamboyant, gay Korean artist, and I am enjoying myself immensely. He awaits the updates on the French affair, and we commiserate as he tells me stories of his lover, never openly admitting it is a man. My creativity is spilling out of cracks and corners and crevices.

On a gondola in Italy last year, I experienced a monumental epiphany—the kind that comes but once in a lifetime. An affluent American man on the train to Venice invited me to dinner that night with his twin twenty year-old daughters. The four of us dined at their posh hotel, the Danieli. Later, over drinks and live classical music in Piazza San Marco, he confessed that it was the first time he had ever asked a woman on a date during an annual trip with the girls, and that he had been concerned about their reaction. I was eleven years his junior, and he had no need to worry; the twins and I hit it off like three peas in a pod.

The following day, they called my *pensione* to invite me out again for an extravagant dinner at the world famous Harry's Bar on the Grand Canal, where my hero, Hemingway, caroused. It was like stepping into an episode of *Lifestyles of the Rich and Famous*. Afterward, I offered to treat them to an evening gondola ride.

Gliding down the black canals, our handsome gondolier, Gabriel, sang *O Sole Mio* to me in an attempt to steal my attention from the American, much to the twins' dismay. It was a dreamlike travel moment, far removed from the monotony of everyday life.

"We think you're really a famous authoress traveling incognito and you're just not tellin' us!" one of the twins blurted out impulsively, in her Southern Virginian drawl.

"No, but I will be." I had no idea where my response came from.

"Will you put us in one of your books?"

"I guarantee it," I declared with certainty.

The Venetian night sky lit up—or so it seemed. An 'ah ha' realization struck; I'd longed to be a writer, but had stuffed the idea deep down into the place where deserted dreams linger. I ate books for breakfast and was dazzled by words, but thought writers were other people, not people like me. Strangers saw the real me long before I'd ever unearthed it out of myself. In that Italian moment, I remembered that I had wanted to write since I was old enough to read Trixie Belden mysteries under weeping willows all summer long.

The vision of 'authoress' has been percolating in my mind since.

Dearest Love,

I very much wanted to send you a fax this morning; unfortunately the telecom in Lisboa is not intercontinental at this moment. Instead, I left a little message on your answering machine. Today, we are separated by 8000 kilometers, but nothing will stop me—I will prove that to you: phone calls, faxes, cards, and letters will continue to follow.

Hold tight my love.

See you soon,

Kisses.

JF

I awaken each morning to calls from Jean-François from cities all over the European continent, and the sound of his voice seductively rouses me from sleep. I am still surprised at his punctuality.

With each conversation, and my daily studies, my French is improving. I want, one day, to be fluent in the language of my ancestors—and in Spanish and Italian—all languages I adore. I am thrilled to be learning a language through and for a lover.

He describes the cities he is working in, and I tell him about my life in Canada. Today, he is in Hamburg, and says that he is not fond of the food in this city, a subject that never bores me. Working long hours, he is grateful for the extra income right now, in light of his divorce proceedings.

No filters in place, I tell everyone I know—my clients, my colleagues, my dental hygienist—even the drycleaner knows that I am in love with a Frenchman who is coming to Canada. I admit to a childish, unabashed anticipation. I have more energy than I can ever remember, and seem to leap through my days. Clients are amused by my enthusiasm. Vicariously adventuring through me, they have always been interested in my life, as I am in theirs, and they look forward to hearing my personal tales when I visit.

For the era in which I entered the world, I was a peculiar little girl. I wanted nothing to do with dolls—except for Barbie. As my sister contentedly washed her little set of dishes in the bathroom sink downstairs, and played mama, not once did I think of babies or motherhood. I wanted nothing more than to grow up as quickly as possible, so I could live out my destiny, minus the confines of dictatorial adults. Perpetually packing up my things in a Huckleberry Finn-style scarf on the end of a stick, and running away from home, my mum would secretly follow me around the neighborhood, until I tired or became frightened, and returned home.

From the ripe age of seven (I think it was the year I decided with certainty to forgo childrearing), I dreamed of the man I would one day meet. Far away from the prairies, in the Rocky Mountains, in a rustic cabin that my dad had rented for a summer vacation, I gazed out the window, and imagined romantic weekends in a cottage nestled in rugged mountains, just like the ones surrounding me. Where these notions came from, I have no idea.

When I learned about menses at Girl Guide camp, it was with wide-eyed fascination for this demonstrable passage, and I impatiently looked for signs of the red rite into womanhood every single day afterwards.

In this, my 35th year, Jean-François feels like that man I have long awaited, while entertaining the jesters and fools, the elusive man I have held in the nucleus of my heart for all these years, while waiting to become that grown-up woman I envisioned so long ago.

I pour a glass of crisp, cold Chardonnay, and lay down tonight with a love letter from Jean-François. Feet on the couch, I settle comfortably on the carpet, and listen to French music while reading the poetic verse, again and again.

Mon Amour,
Aujourd'hui nous sommes samedi et c'est notre dernier ...

Wild ideas have begun to infiltrate my thoughts, and a program I have just watched about France has further fueled them. Jean-François and I have initiated long conversations, daydreaming over what we shall do about this situation. Willing to move to Canada, he could get a transfer, but the idea of this Euro-steeped man being gratified by our godforsaken winters and gastronomic wasteland seems improbable. I cannot visualize his brazen presence in the mundaneness of a suburban Canadian life.

I imagine myself leaving my life behind to go to France.

It is at once a terrifying idea, juxtaposed with exhilaration. My truest self is about this, to the core—romance and all things foreign. But in spite of my intrinsic wanderlust, I have become, paradoxically, root-bound. It is not a trait I was born with; it is a fear-based byproduct of cancer. It is an intense need for some semblance of security.

At the time of my diagnosis, my husband and I had been renting a cozy house in a convenient central location. Just as I began five weeks of radiation treatments, the landlord listed the house for sale. He paraded a host of potential buyers through the sanctity of our home, disrupting my much needed rest and tranquility. Feeling exposed, I vowed we would imminently have a home of our own, so that no one could ever again invade our privacy in such a manner.

With dogged determination post-recovery, I worked long hours after my day job at my sideline business to design, create, and sell jewelry; sometimes working into the night, to complete the many orders I received. My husband didn't think we could do it, but when I set my mind to something with unwavering clarity, and white-hot intention, I often succeed.

It was not long before we had accumulated enough money for a down payment on our first home. This house is that home, and I have a profound attachment to what it represents: a safe haven from the perils of the world. I have created a sweet, serene sanctuary, one that I would find hard to leave behind.

My Dearest Wanda,

Another day ends—one day closer to you. I bring to you very good news: I reviewed my work calendar for the month of August, and I can come from the 9th for ten days. All I need do is find a flight, and I promise you that nothing, nor anyone, will prevent me. I need your love.

This started like a game, but today I understand that you are a part of my life, and I want us to continue. It seems unjust to be separated from you, when my desire is to be by your side every day. I think of you hourly. I have the picture I took of you in the Barrio Alto in your little black dress with the big yellow sunflowers. I spend time looking at this sweet picture of you laughing wholeheartedly, and you are beautiful. And I tell myself, if it is our wish, it is up to us to find a way to be together.

Do not doubt me, Wanda. I promise you, once more, that I am doing all I can to be with you quickly. It is necessary that I prospect maximally for a job there, if that is what you desire (with your help: English makes it so).

The vacation with my son is sailing smoothly; he is a good boy, but the first days of the holiday were cold and it rained heavily.

I have a lot to tell you about my plans, but all is so uncertain that I am scared of mentioning it, yet I am thoroughly convinced about fulfilling them. Wanda, be faithful, wait for me, our life together depends on it.

Love,
Jean-François

♥

Le Français has just booked a flight to Canada for his August birthday. Will we feel the same connection and love-drunkenness in my country as we did in the exotic environment of a sultry and festive June in Lisbon? I have a quaint business studio apartment in the trendy Mission district of Calgary, and I will take him there. After I tend to sales calls in the outlying area, it will be a good opportunity for him to see the Rocky Mountains and Southern Alberta. We will discover more about each other, and have a better idea if we wish to move forward in this French affair.

My Love,

The "D" day gets closer. When you get this card, there will be two or three days left before I can finally squeeze you again in my arms. I anxiously await that moment. I am in a hurry.

I kiss you tenderly.

See you, oh so soon.

Jean-François

August

When love is not madness, it is not love.
—Pedro Calderón de la Barca

A DOZEN LONG-STEMMED RED ROSES IN HAND, I ARRIVE AT
the airport early. I have packaged myself into a gift: bold Russian
Red Mac lipstick, polished and pedicured toes, and a delightful
new white dress that is, as well, dotted in big red roses.

My home is prepped to perfection. Even though I abhor
housework, I am in a phase of freakish tidiness; everything is
impeccable, and in order. Large bouquets of fresh cut flowers
don the kitchen table and fill the bedroom. The fridge is brim
full with gourmet treats and bottles of champagne. Even the
oven is scrubbed to a sparkle. I also bribed the neighbor kids to
cut the lawn and pick the weeds, which I hate to do because of
the bastard spiders.

I have planned a surprise birthday party for my lover on the
weekend. Everyone has been whipped into a frenzy by my excitement, and they are now itching to meet him—a good excuse to
get my crew of family and friends all over at the same time.

I feel the same fluttering sensations I felt as a child, when it was
time to open gifts at Christmas. Even now, I insist on continuing
the tradition of opening a single gift on Christmas Eve with my
family, one that I created as an impatient young girl.

Tonight is Christmas Eve in August.

I scan the crowds shuffling out of the customs gate, disheveled and tired. Families exit with crabby little children straggling behind. Old couples meander hand in hand. Honeymooners laugh, arms entwined. Girls glowing from their sojourn to Paris race away with their luggage in tow.

I resist stamping my feet.

Where is he?

Anticipation is building so strongly, I feel I could spontaneously combust.

Finally, he exits the sliding doors.

Good God.

He is so tall and striking and French looking and he evokes a red lava rush through my insides. My smile could light the Eiffel Tower. I attempt decorum, but we both run to each other. He grabs me, lifts me off the ground, and smothers me in kisses. Stepping back to look at me, he grins, and we both speak at the same time, our faces flushed.

Standing at the carousel, we embrace again and again. After retrieving his luggage, we await a heavy case of Alsatian wine, arriving from special cargo.

"We must celebrate. For your friends and your *mère* and *père* when we meet!"

Driving the twenty-five kilometers to my home, laughing and kissing, we barely contain our madness, both with the same thing in mind.

After depositing his cases on the living room floor, I grab a bottle of champagne and two iced flutes, and we race upstairs, *tout de suite.* Kissing me deeply, with strong hands on my waist, he draws me tightly into his body. I am flooded with recollections of what is to come. Disinterested in the champagne, we fall onto the bed instead, without need for spirits. The birds chirp in their sunset chatter outside my window, and a light summer breeze blows the white gauzy canopy around the brass frame.

I know this man. I know him profoundly, for eternity. I don't know why I know this; I feel it in the recesses of my psyche. It is not silly or stupid. It is as real as the ground I walk on every day. I am somewhere else with him—another place and a different time.

He doesn't just make love to me; he envelops my senses and occupies me. Traces of resistance I have held over the years, the slight withholding of trust—even with my husband—have vanished. Completely disarmed, no fortress walls are left standing. I don't care, and I have acquiesced, without argument from any part of my being.

Nibbling my neck, he weaves French love words into my hair. "*Je t'aime*," he whispers, and I spiral. Lines blur between reality and fantasy.

We fit.

We meld.

I am scorched, liquescent as hot butter. He loves me on fire—this is what human bodies were built for. *La petite mort*, the French call it. I die many small deaths tonight.

After, he rests his champagne flute on my belly, and twirls and swirls his fingers over my body, making my already electrified skin quiver. He slips a piece of dark French chocolate into my mouth, doubling the sensation in my love-drugged mind.

We chatter unendingly, the way lovers do, with too many things to say and never enough time.

Exhausted by the profound pleasure, and the relief after such crazed expectancy, I burrow into his body and fall into a deep sleep, safe and spent.

The day has arrived for the grand *fête*, the gathering where everyone will meet my French paramour. We have been busily preparing the food together. Jean-François knows his way around the kitchen, and did not exaggerate when he said he could cook.

Last night, he whipped up a simple, divine meal: a green salad with a delicate mustard vinaigrette, perfectly pan-fried steak *au buerre*, Provence herbed potatoes, and a crusty baguette we picked up from the European bakery, paired with a bodacious bottle of Beaujolais Nouveau. We dined on the patio under a starry night.

Friends and family are arriving, the noise level rising as the Alsatian wine flows. It is a flawless summer evening, with people spread out on the lawn, clustered around flowerbeds, and spilling over the patio. A group of men hover around the barbeque, and my father is in a deep discussion in French with Jean-François. Watching them warms me.

Jean-François seduces everyone. He is a charming man with big presence. My girlfriends discreetly poke me, with an effusive 'thumbs up.' As I pull another bottle of wine from the fridge, my mum walks into the kitchen and says, with uncharacteristic chutzpah, if I don't go to France with him, *she* will.

Merriment fills the night sky, as we eat, drink, and savor the uncommon late hour balminess. The last of our guests leave at 3 a.m. and we fall into bed, laughing, our happiness quotient overflowing from the heart-swelling, celebratory evening.

We have fallen into long and intricate discussions of what to do about us. He has tenure, and offers to request a transfer to Canada. This is a pivotal moment—my chance to live my long-held dream. My stomach aflutter, I tell him I want to go to France.

Jean-François asks what I will do for work. I say I will seek some type of travel writing assignments when we go on his varied contracts to other countries.

"But you've never written before. How can you do that?" he asks with his engineer-brained logic.

"I don't know, but I know I can do it. I really want to, and I think I can find a way."

Not convinced that this is a viable thing for me to pursue, he drops the subject. I know that I will not be hired in Europe in a sales and marketing capacity, without the proper language skills, and I am itching to shift into a creative, more feminine work life.

The sun is streaming in through the bedroom window of my studio suite in Calgary, and Jean-François is wrapped around my body. Half of my business life is spent here; so much time that I was one of the Sheraton Hotel's top ten clients for a number of years. Because of that status, I was always given superior suites with a spectacular view of the mountains. Last year, my boss asked if I would prefer an apartment, instead of staying at the hotel, and I agreed to it. Like an indulgent father, he gave me a generous allowance to furnish it. The tiny apartment is cozy and comfortable, with my style stamped on it.

With my workweek completed, Jean-François and I will travel for the weekend. Since he has arrived, my body has been in a spin and butterflies within. Two days ago, I began having severe cramps, and now I am in so much pain I must visit a doctor at the nearby medi-center.

With genuine concern, Jean-François presses me for the diagnosis on our walk to the drugstore for an over-the-counter remedy. I do not want to reveal my silliness; the doctor checked me over for under a minute, and asked when I'd last been to the bathroom.

In my excitement—and also a ridiculous female perception that one needs to hide bodily functions around a man—I realized I hadn't had a bowel movement for days. My penance is the liquid 'dynamite' I am now forced to drink. I am mortified, but men typically don't see such things that way.

It is a cloudless day en route to Banff. I never tire of the majesty of the mountains, and surprise vistas around curves and over hilltops can still take my breath away. The energy here is calming, and the strength and solidity of the terrain is grounding. Jean-François is duly impressed with the Canadian Rockies.

In spite of the language barrier, we are never at a loss for lively conversation, and no moment with him is lackluster. Stopping in each small shop in search of gifts for his son, we look over polished stones, and memorabilia, and t-shirts with grizzly bears. He is ever so selective in choosing just the right thing, debating what he should buy.

On a rooftop patio, we soak up the sun's yellow afternoon light over a cappuccino and pastries, and then drive to a lake that I love to visit, one tucked away from the crowds.

A gopher makes its way to our blanket to eat leftover croissants out of our hands, and Jean-François tells me more about the countryside in France, about European politics, about the things he and his son do when he is at home.

Walking hand in hand around the milky-turquoise lake at sunset, a herd of mountain goats arrive, the baby wearily edging to the water for a drink. As the moon peeks over a cliff out of the dusk, we head home.

Near the grocery store, Jean-François turns the wrong way down a one-way street. He has insisted on driving on our ventures out of town, which suits me fine, but I don't know French well enough to explain the rules of the road.

"*Arrêt!*" I yell.

He looks at me quizzically, and keeps driving.

"*Non, non! Arrêt! … S'il vous plaît—maintenant, Jean-François!*"

A car heads directly toward us, and it is now that he comprehends my pleas. He quickly pulls over, and I slap his arm with a grin, asking him to please listen to me when driving in Canada.

In Safeway, he catches me around the waist in an aisle, and kisses me deeply, and an elderly woman behind us nearly crashes her cart into a display of baked beans. Even grocery shopping is an escapade.

Tonight he is cooking, and wants fish for dinner. Understandably, he is disappointed with the selection, and grabs a package to read the fine print.

"*Non! Mais non!*" he cries. "*Imitation peixe? Impossible!*"

He waves a plastic pack of imitation crab in the air.

"Why on Earth would anyone make imitation fish? There is real fish everywhere! Who eats this? Are they *crazy*?" he says in French, gesticulating in disbelief.

I giggle madly, out of breath and almost falling over, while a nearby shopper pretends to examine a package of sausages, but is watching Jean-François. He is noisy, and not a man who blends into the beige-scape of Calgary, Alberta, Canada. His intensity burns brightly no matter where he goes, and nothing escapes his attention.

We set out a candlelit picnic on the hardwood floor, with the red gingham tablecloth and napkins that I, thankfully, remembered to pack, sitting on my duvet and drinking wine until late. He asks many questions about my job and my life on the road. He wants to know what I think, and how I feel about life, love, and God.

We don't want to close our eyes, to miss a moment of each other. Soon, he will be returning to France, and I can't think about it. I want him to stay. Naturally, the sexual element—the lust that makes my brain swim in a primordial soup, and my body vibrate electrically—is intoxicating. But there is much more. There is a tangling of our souls—an ease—a naked and raw understanding of the other.

Love hangs sweetly in the air as we succumb to sleep, our fingers intertwined, our bodies softly surrendered.

The night my husband proposed, he had prepared a colossal fondue, with an exquisitely paired wine, and had a Chris de Burgh concert playing in the background. He was uncharacteristically fidgety and nervous and I still did not clue in. The very last thing I expected was a marriage proposal.

I had just returned from a 24-day trip to the Greek Isles, and he declared that he never wanted to be without me again for that long. He loved me, and wanted to be with me forever. Would I marry him? So far away was my mind from thoughts of marriage that, when he placed a tiny blue velvet box on the table, and I found a twinkling, pear-shaped carat diamond inside, I thought it was a prank. I laughed—somewhat hysterically. Then I cried. I did not answer for a long while and, with a face that belied panic, he asked if I was going to reply.

I'd had absolutely no intention of getting married anytime soon. I loved him, but it had not even occurred to me. I looked into his eyes—and saw his heart and soul; I knew in that moment that if I said no, we were over. I did not want us to end, and so I said yes.

Being engaged was terrifying for the first weeks afterwards. I would stare at the ring on my finger in disbelief, twirling it around and around absently. Slowly, I grew fond of the idea. The word 'wife' would rattle around in my head, and I began to embrace the concept of matrimony.

Our honeymoon might well have been one of the best on record, all orchestrated by my new husband. Once we were married, the advantages appeared to be rich and life enhancing. But ten months in, the honeymoon phase was rudely interrupted by cancer. After my recovery, something was amiss.

Too late, I discovered a well-hidden secret, which was the source of immense inner turmoil for this man—a teenage-hood that read like a Shakespearian tragedy, complete with betrayal, murder, and suicide. A well-meaning relative, who saw trouble brewing in our marriage, leaked the story. My husband had no plans of sharing his horrific history with me, and had intended to die with the secret.

Although he awoke early every morning like a chirping meadowlark, and not once raised his voice, or ever said a rude word to me, he was in a constant state of denial and underlying angst, which he numbed with alcohol.

I loved my husband, and always will on some level. He was highly compatible with the part of me harboring worn and ingrained familial patterns that permeate my DNA. Our relationship began on a dysfunctional note: me accommodating someone with a serious problem—me loving too much in spite of crazy-making. He was a good man with a soft heart but, unfortunately, a severely broken one. I had a gut-wrenching realization that this was a problem no amount of love or tender care could mend.

Was cancer going to give me five more years, or fifty? I had to consider my health and peace of mind, no matter my affection and love for him. When he made it clear he had no intentions of dealing with the pain of the past, nor the addiction, there was lamentably nothing left for me to do but end the marriage prematurely.

Now, I have already flirted with the outlandish fantasy of marrying this Frenchman. Even though I lean toward a phobia of commitment, I long to marry again. I loved being a couple; cooking and entertaining together; having a travel buddy; the warmth of a beloved one to snuggle with on movie nights. What a detour it would be to learn another language through full-on French immersion; to eat first-rate food, and drink wine right from the vineyards; to dig into my ancestral roots and search for Mont St-Hilaire in the countryside of France. And to experience the culture shock of living near a small French village, with a man infinitely different than any I have ever known.

He alluded to it before he went back home. Yes, the idea of marriage excites me.

Situated in a golden wheat field amongst orderly rows of round bails, Donna and I are out in the countryside on a photo shoot. In a wanton mood, I chose to wear a pair of brief jean shorts, and a cleavage-revealing, off-the-shoulder top, with a black cowboy hat, and suede cowboy boots. I plan to surprise Jean-François with authentically Albertan photos, via post.

A warm, late August afternoon, the air holds an ever so slight hint of autumn. I climb the bails, scratching my bare legs, and almost tumbling off, as Donna directs me on alluring poses, like a professional. We are both enjoying this unique excursion, neither of us having done such a thing before. Covered in dust and dry bits of hay, we take leave after hours of snapping rolls of film. The sun has begun its descent, and we chatter our way down country roads, heading back to the city for a much-deserved dinner out.

Donna stops in for a quick glass of wine afterwards, and then I am left alone to my musings. Many is the old woman who keeps a secret, like a cherished treasure, of that one love she has never forgotten. She knows every woman should experience the feeling once in a lifetime, no matter where it leads. Had she been obliged to leave the man behind, or opted not to take the chance on love, the sorrow stayed—sometimes buried, sometimes blatant.

I suspected that my French grandmother, whom I never met, had a furtive man in her past. From my father's stories, it was apparent that she was an acutely frustrated and angry woman, and I asked him one day if he knew of a secret lost love she might have hidden away. It was not so mysterious: on her dresser sat a photo of a man she sang to, and of, he told me. She flagrantly flaunted him in front of her husband and children, and died at mid-life from hypertension. After the glamour of Montreal, and the love she was forced to leave behind, I surmise that her misery at living in a backward, rural town, with a man who rarely spoke, sent her blood pressure to the boiling point, and her heart into splinters.

Possibly, this is too high of a high. Yet surely, it is one of God's greatest gifts to human beings. Monotony is washed away. Insignificant details disappear. The world, not figuratively, but literally, looks more vivid and vibrant. Like a silly commercial, love like this makes me want to dance in a field of flowers. I am wildly in love with life—and with everyone.

Who would not want to feel like this, man or woman? Alive to the core, blood singing through veins, with access—at last—to an elusive glimpse of ecstasy.

September

If you can make a woman laugh, you can make her do anything.
—Marilyn Monroe

BLUE SMOKE FILLS THE FRONT OF THE ROOM AS PIERRE, the owner of the paper company we represent, lights a thick Cuban cigar in the midst of a sales meeting. He sets the stogie down in an ashtray and it smolders. It is unconscionable. One of those balding, podgy types in an expensive but wrinkled suit, he thinks he is all that and a bag of potato chips, because he has money.

Au contraire, monsieur.

I glare at Ron, my boss, but he avoids eye contact. Clearing my throat, I shuffle papers, a red-hot anger pulsing through me. Trapped in a small conference room, this insufferable man has the audacity to subject us to his noxious habit in a business setting.

Since my arrival into the hustle of Toronto for our annual assembly, I have been ready to jump out of my skin, and onto the next plane home. This display exemplifies the life of a sales representative. I despise meetings, and I am tired of having no voice, so to speak. For years, I have been subjected to the whims of idiosyncratic managers who, in reality, have absolutely no education on how to manage people effectively. Ron is a wonderful and fair man, but even he kowtows to the heads of the companies we represent. Currently, we work with sixteen manufacturers;

that means I must kiss the butts of *sixteen* different managers, not including my three bosses.

A thousand trade shows, a million miles traveled, and far too many of these dry, pointless meetings. If these men had a spark of imagination and true vision, it would not be so unbearable. But they are working from a worn out paradigm that is dying. The world is on the cusp of a sweeping evolution, and we are still slogging it out with antiquated tactics, and a dearth of creativity. With the possibility of transitioning into a new, better-suited life in Europe dangling in front of me, all of my heretofore-suppressed irritation bubbles to the surface.

While Pierre drones on robotically, my mind drifts. The ringing of a phone on the credenza breaks my reverie, startling everyone. Clyde, one of my bosses, grabs it, and his thick moustache contorts, his face in a red fury, as he signals *me* to come to the phone. Calls never come in while we are in conference, and this is either an emergency, or a faux pas.

It is Jean-François.

How in the hell did he find me in this room?

Whispering, I tell him that I am in a business meeting, and it is not an appropriate time to talk. I speak in broken French, and must repeat myself. My face is pink, and growing hotter, as my colleagues listen in. Although it is highly unprofessional to receive a call during a meeting such as this, I am secretly pleased that I am the reason Pierre's insipid spiel has been interrupted. In business, I am always the picture of paranoia and proper behavior and, frankly, I feel mutinous.

Four more days. Four long days of making inane small chat over dinners and drinks, of listening to stifling strategies and dull pitches, while my body longs for France.

My Love,

In my life, you alone have been able to make me tremble with joy and love. You know we will succeed in our life together. That is my deepest desire, and I want you to know you make me happy. When we live together, you will understand me better. I promise you that once the time comes, I will build you a cozy nest, where you can be happy with me until the end of our days.

Every time you face low moments, I will be there.

Every time you are sad, I will be there.

Every time you have aches or are in pain, I will be there too.

Without you I am nothing—my life belongs to you.

A kiss from one who adores you.

I have been tossed into an intensive autumn back-to-work schedule. Spring bookings are already in full swing, and a round of long road trips lies ahead. Faxes fly in and out of my tiny home office at all hours, and I seem to be constantly resolving one problem or another.

Jean-François calls every day. He keeps me amused with stories of his business trips, and I do my best to speak in fragmented French. We have firmly made the decision that we want to be together. Now we are in discussions about moving. Who will leave their homeland, and who will stay?

Born at one minute to midnight, in a cold prairie city on a December's eve, I have lived what has long felt like a displacement, but I have adapted. It is not that I feel Canada is a bad place—not at all. But just as some men feel they are born as women, I was placed in a country with a different sensibility than the people around me—a girl with a Bohemian Latina soul.

A chance meeting at twelve years old gave me some insight into my true nature, when I met an Italian girl named Maria. Our families had both recently arrived from other cities, and were temporarily renting downtown apartments. Within weeks, serendipitously, both families bought homes two blocks apart, in a muddy suburb still under construction.

When I entered their alien world, it was like coming home. Their house was always filled with loud people speaking singsong Italian, hands waving madly in the air to make a point. Dinners were an event, with heaping bowls of pasta smothered in mouthwatering meat sauce, large square pizzas made from scratch, and all kinds of food I had never eaten before. Maria's brothers and cousins would teach me nasty Italian words, and laugh hysterically when I would repeat them in front of their parents.

Years later, in Greece, while I meandered the mazes of Mykonos, I imagined myself pulling a '*Shirley Valentine*', staying on a white-washed Cycladic island for a season. I would sail in the turquoise Aegean Sea, hike through olive groves, and return home with brown breasts from sunning all summer long on the topless beaches.

Riding through the streets in Italy on rented Vespas, I felt a tremendous affinity to the ancient cities. I fantasized about what it would be like to have an apartment in Florence. I could study Italian, and eat *osso buco* with heaps of *tagliatelle* drenched in pesto. I would visit vineyards and drink Chianti, and gorgeous Italian men—whose national pastime is the pursuit of women—would chase me.

Every time I think of inviting Jean-François to live here with me, I cannot imagine it. He has had *déplacements* in every country in Europe—all over the world for that matter—and his tastes are sophisticated. When I envision him here, I see a man lost.

On the other hand, when I consider leaving Canada to test French life with Jean-François, I am awash in exhilaration, and I know I would adapt there better than he here.

My job offers a multitude of benefits. It is hard and demanding work, but it is the best career move I have taken, and I am making a reputable name for myself in the industry. Yet, even in light of the full life I have here, the lure is powerfully enticing and grows each day. I am close to telling him I choose to go to live with him.

Oh, so close.

Armed with a new jumbo-sized French dictionary, a set of language CDs, and a book called *Culture Shock! France*, I study. The book has detailed information about attitudes, cultural mores, and basic insights on how not to look like a complete oaf, if you are relocating. I have been listening to the French CDs on my road trips, and I am improving in my conversations with Jean-François. I do, however, still need help interpreting his letters, and I'm sure a lot of the nuances are lost in translation.

Long nights over good wine, I've had deep discussions with girlfriends about what to do. We have debated the pros and cons of staying or leaving, and contemplated all of the ramifications. None of them has ever had to make such a decision, and it is all conjecture. They are excited for me, yet at the same time don't want me to leave Canada forever.

October

You know you're in love when you can't fall asleep, because reality is finally better than your dreams.
—Dr. Seuss

'*L'AMOUR EXISTE ENCORE ...*'

Tristful, I sit on the floor listening to French chanteuses. Alas, I have made the decision to move to France. With things now set in motion, I labor to unearth my essence from this place, to release the tendrils I have wrapped around this little two-story house. It has been my tranquil refuge in turbulent seas. Countless Sunday mornings, I have regenerated my mind and rejuvenated my body in the big brass bed, tucked under the massive breakfast tray (a Christmas gift handcrafted by my ex-husband), reading magazines, and savoring slow brunches with steaming lattes.

Having fallen in love with the Greek Islands, I asked my husband to design the kitchen to look like a Mykonian home when we moved in. He white-stuccoed the walls, painted the cupboards, and trimmed everything in pine, as the Greeks do. We made it fresh and new with accents of blue, like the Cycladic homes I stayed in. Lovingly, we manicured the lawn, planted the flowerbeds, and built a small garden. Both of us tidy by nature, it was an immaculate abode that we filled with family and friends.

When we divorced, he knew what this house represented to me, and my staying caused no arguments. Following on my heels, my mum went through a tumultuous divorce, and stayed with me for a period of rest and regrouping. Later, when I recovered from back surgery, my home served as a healing sanctuary.

Tonight, I lie down with my head beside the stereo, and sob. It is not easy for me to let go. I crave a new, exciting pathway. I want to experience life in Europe. I love Jean-Francois. But I need to mourn the loss of my life, as I have known it to be.

My dad has dropped by for a visit while I painstakingly sort through the pile of boxes in my basement. After careful deliberation, I have decided to sell my house, my car, and most of my furniture. He finds the work I must do to prepare for this venture discouraging and daunting. Now that I have made these choices, I am steadfast in my anticipation of a new life, and I forge through the tasks with military-style stringency.

I have purchased everything I shall need for six months in France: shampoo, assorted lotions, make-up, tampons, film, writing paper, toothbrushes—all of the incidentals—and will soon be shipping them off to Jean-François' home for my arrival.

Steaming tea in hand, my dad asks philosophical questions about my plans, and how I came to make this life-altering choice. Not the type to accept a quick one-liner, he wants to know the psychology behind what I am doing. As I sift through crammed boxes, we discuss the positives and negatives, hypothesizing about what this trip may bring.

Hours later, after enough of the tedium, we head upstairs and onto the patio for fresh air and pastrami sandwiches. Surveying my small yard with its lush trees, now orange and red with autumn's turn, I note the flowerbeds wilting in preparation for a dormant winter.

This is not an easy transition for someone whose blood is laced with sentimentality. My parents hold onto things like a drowning man would a whirling life preserver caught in the undertow. While the rest of the world saw it from the beginning, including my six-year-old self, it took them thirty-two years to come to the conclusion they should divorce. We are a clan of alarmists and reactionaries.

Each day, I must override these familial tendencies and tell myself, as Christopher Robin told Pooh, that I am braver than I believe, and stronger than I seem, and smarter than I think.

Never having been to France before, I only know of it from hearsay and from Jean-François' stories. I will be fully steeped in the language, with no choice but to learn. I look forward to the scent of lavender, and the sunflower field vistas, and antiquated stone farmhouses. I will take French cooking classes, and we will create meals together. We will make love under a full moon, just as we did by the castle in Lisbon.

I shall begin my writing venture with thought-provoking articles about the places we will travel to on his contracts, investigating and recording while he is at work. If I remain after the six months, I will see about an odd job. With enough funds to keep me afloat for my leave, it will all come together.

Jean-François' son spends weekends with him when he is not away on business. Never having had a moment of motherly impulses, it will be a different experience for me, but he is a teen and well aware that I am coming. A daughter might be a challenge, if she was possessive, but I'm sure Antoine and I will get on.

The imaginary is now real, and has come in a most unexpected way—and I am scared. Petrified, actually. But each day I take the steps, tearing down the bricks and mortar of my life, bit by bit, one step closer to France. I have more mettle than I knew of; my wanderlust has a highly influential soul of its own.

Thinking possibly it was a case of nerves, stomach pains and discomfort drove me to go see Dr. Ross. Since we were both in our early twenties—when he looked remarkably like a sixteen year old Doogie Houser MD—I have been his patient. Not overly concerned, he said that if I had come in with an intuitive feeling about something erroneous, he would be remiss if he did not send me off with a requisition for an ultrasound.

Much to my utter annoyance, I have gallstones. These maladies never seem to end, and I am only thirty-five years old. Consulting with the same surgeon who performed my lumpectomy, he advised me that I may be okay for a while, but should I need emergency surgery in France, it would require a more invasive technique, and would entail a large gash across my stomach. If I do it now, I will be able to have microscopic surgery.

I do not want to set foot in one more hospital. However, a dramatic emergency in Europe doesn't sound appealing, so I have reluctantly opted for the preventive measure.

I appreciate accolades for positive accomplishments, yet I am beginning to wonder if this medical shite is a subconscious ploy for attention. Just in case, I have instructed all of my friends and family to refrain from acknowledging this latest procedure. No cards, no gifts, no flowers, no condolence-like visits—I want nothing to reinforce a potential payoff to illness.

Out of the hospital, and having recovered quickly, it was a successful tactic. I was determined to participate in a joint garage sale to earn proceeds toward my trip to France. I have declared the intention to sell enough of my basement excavations to cover my plane ticket.

The amount of junk I have amassed is absurd. Packing my car to the rooftop, I make my way to the suburbs at the opposite end of the city to set up at my friend Leslie's weekend event. Much to my mystification, the first thing to sell is a damaged bust of King Tut.

By the day's end, I am ecstatic to discover that I have met my goal, in spite of a sneaky garage sale thief stealing an expensive safe. I have $1300 cash in hand, the exact cost of my plane ticket to France.

My Love,

I have so much to tell you, so happy to know that you, too, are ready for our union. I have a head full of plans.

In three weeks, you will be in my bed. I think about that without ceasing ... I know it will be so sweet, my dear Wanda. Your body is made for mine. With you, I get to love to the end of my fingers.

You are my sun; let me love you for a whole lifetime.

Avec Amour,

Jean-François

A rich brocade tablecloth with matching napkins catches my eye. I have been plotting out a magnificent Christmas for Jean-François and his son, who will be with his papa for a part of the season. I have bought Jean-François a sturdy Swiss watch, a well-tailored shirt that will suit him perfectly, and an assortment of small gifts. I spend many hours shopping for both of them, not for the love of the activity, but for the love of him.

I purchase the tablecloth, along with some Canadiana Christmas décor. My bags will be absurdly heavy, but I cannot quash my crazed enthusiasm for the chance to create a Christmas extraordinaire in France. All three of us women in my immediate family are prone to overdoing things, if you can call it that. Always phenomenal food on the table, and a welcoming home filled with festive décor, my mum has given us solid traditions of whatever season or occasion it may be, and my sister and I have wholeheartedly adopted her love of giving, and of celebration.

Holding a steady buzz all week, I arrive at my grand farewell party, my nervous energy skyrocketing into overdrive. My best friends have booked a charming downtown café, and it is filled with noisy well-wishing family, friends, and acquaintances. Wine flows and food is devoured. Friends joust to record their silly advice and heartfelt bon voyages on a video-cam that has been set up in a corner. My cheeks hurt from laughing, but I also fight to control the lump in my throat, and to restrain the tears that threaten to overwhelm me. It is a bittersweet night; I am high-test espresso, percolating over my French adventure, and I can't wait to see Jean-François again in his own environment. But at the same time, my heart recoils at leaving behind my family, and such beloved soul sisters and sweet friendships.

Lynnette is the most affected by my decision; she has confessed that she feels I am abandoning her. It took tremendous courage for her to leave her husband with their adopted daughter, and we have been a tag-team, fiercely supporting and uplifting the other in a rare bond that comes with need, and reciprocal caring and love.

I do have a lofty plan though. I envision a future where Lynnette, Shari, Donna, and my dear sister will visit to take jaunts about Europe, while Jean-François is on contract elsewhere. I imagine them staying for one-month stints in our home in the countryside, driving through Provence, and gorging on French wine and farm-fresh cheese, cooking together and dining al fresco. And I intend to be back here often, to keep my friendships strong.

Lynnette is here though, uncertain about her future as a single mother with a troubled child, and I am flying off on an escapade, for an indeterminate amount of time. In the midst of my love tempest, I cannot completely understand her feelings. I am too swept up—the dream of a lifetime is unfolding, and I am on an epic high.

Taking down the remainder of my collection of Egyptian paraphernalia and artifacts, I wrap them quickly. I tuck in photos and tape up the boxes. I am surprised at the ease of the final packing up, the disassembling of my life in this little two-story house.

There are the happy marital memories: the quick efficiency of my husband renovating our new nest to my wishes, and the warm feeling of being safely ensconced in a home of our own. There was the late-night revelry at our many dinner parties, and the weekend family barbeques. Also, the slow Sunday mornings of eggs benny with frothy lattes in bed, lingering together under the thick duvet.

But there are the bad too: the agony of pacing into the early morning hours until my husband would arrive home, a drunken driver who could have easily killed an innocent person—or himself. Then the nights rendered sleepless, with suspicions of infidelity, subsumed with the confusion of questioning my own intense intuition as nonsense.

I have not had enough time here to grow roots so entangled that they won't let me leave this home behind. It has meant many things to me, but I can now move forward, onto the next chapter of my life.

November

When all is said and done, the weather and love are the two elements about which one can never be sure.
—Alice Hoffman

AWAKENED BY THE GNAWING IN MY STOMACH, I HAVE RISEN exceptionally early in the darkness. Tomorrow, I leave for France. Outside my window, the frozen landscape mirrors the ice coursing through my veins. Shaky, my body is filled with a hum of anxiety. I have confided to no one that Jean-François has not called this week. While carrying on with the many last minute details and farewells, my gut screams that something is seriously amiss.

Since we met, Jean-François has been impeccable with his word. My mind regurgitates and perseverates; he has sent a cascade of letters filled with promises, and has never missed a daily call, no matter his location. Together, we have made these plans meticulously and methodically, with rationality. As each day has brought me one day closer to leaving, I toss around a barrage of scenarios and potential motives for his deafening silence. I review conversations for clues.

I cannot tell anyone; I must be patient. There has to be an explanation—a sensible one. However, harboring this sickening secret is silent hell.

With nothing in the house to eat, I venture out for breakfast. Mustering all of my will to calm myself over coffee, I cannot quell my angst to get back home, to await his call. Surely it will come before my flight.

Cruelly, the day ticks on in silence. My bags are packed—the only things that remain out are the toiletries required for the morning. The house echoes in emptiness, exacerbating my dread. All that occupies the space are my suitcases and a sleeping bag, so I repack again to keep my hands busy. But my mind will not quiet.

In truth, I know that when women rationalize a man's erratic or bad behavior—when they hang their hearts onto the notion that something unforeseen, or unexpected, or valid, is the cause— the explanation is enormously balanced on the side of unacceptability. An accident is highly improbable—a vague possibility, but not likely.

As each hour passes, I sink deeper, spiraling down, down, down into confusion, trying not to descend into a pit of full-blown panic.

After dusk, my parents arrive to take me for a farewell dinner. This is a moment I have not looked forward to. We are a melodramatic lot, and I topple the scales with my behemoth highs, and desolate lows. They are happy for me—yes—but the idea of not knowing when I will return has them both edgy with sadness. Aside from my own melancholy at leaving behind all of the people I love so fiercely, my nerves dangle from a fine thread.

Still, no call has come.

Having recently gone through a '*War of the Roses*' divorce, the conversation is strained between my mum and dad. Drawing from my best sales techniques, I paste on a fake happy face, and talk of my upcoming trip with feigned enthusiasm. I can barely swallow a bite of food past the lump in my throat.

What if he does not call? Will I land across the world to find myself alone at an airport with no place to go?

I try to focus on the conversation while fear spins through my body and wrenches my bowels.

Back at my cavernous house, I mask my apprehension as I walk past my parents to check the answering machine.

No blinking light.

Lingering over mindless chatter while we say our final fare-wells, the phone rings, reverberating loudly on the bare walls. My heart bounces erratically against my ribcage.

"Hello," I murmur, almost choking.

"Allo? Wanda?"

He talks softly, asking inane niceties, *en Français*. I answer, all the while my body aching in anticipation of the explanation for his vanishing act. He pauses for a long moment, and then speaks his next words almost inaudibly. With a rush of adren-aline coursing through my body like the force of Iguazú Falls, they deafen me.

"Don't come now. Now is not a good time," he says in a conspiratorial whisper.

After our daily phone calls, and many love letters mapping out our future together, his words are inconceivable.

I stop breathing.

A maelstrom swirls, picking up thoughts and questions and hurling them violently against the inside of my head.

"*Pardon*?" I finally say, in French.

He speaks of a job that he has accepted in India. I remind him of our agreement: he will take no contracts outside of Europe for six months. He further explains, but my mind had gone blank, with a pounding that drowns out his voice. I ask him to repeat what he has just said, and I will myself to listen closely this time. I remind him of our written-in-stone plans. Still, he says he must take this contract.

Convincing myself that I have lost something in translation, I ask my father to speak to him, to see if I have misunderstood.

They begin a lengthy discussion in French. I hear my dad say, "You know she has sold her house?"

"You know she has taken leave of her job for six months?"

"You know she has a plane ticket for *tomorrow*?"

The conversation comes to a close, and my father looks at me with sickening regret. He hands me the phone in slow motion.

"You understood correctly."

Putting the receiver to my ear, I tell my lover that I have nothing left to do, but to leave Canada for Europe. I don't know if he will be there or not, but I will be on that plane tomorrow, traveling to an unknown destiny.

Mumbling a good-bye, I hang up.

Engulfed in tears, and the searing pain of disbelief, I slide down the wall, gripping my gut. The words my parents speak are indecipherable. Asking them to go, they reluctantly leave me in the barren house, yesterday's ebullient daughter now a sobbing heap on the floor.

Snow pelts the windows, my soul as cold as the ice forming on the panes. As alone as I have ever been, I wrap myself in the sleeping bag, falling into a fitful sleep of dragons and nightmares reminiscent of childhood.

Friends have come to fetch me for the airport, and a gaggle of girls surround me at a table near the gate for my final farewell. I perform a sham adieu full of cheer—one worthy of a Meryl Streep Oscar.

The façade falls the instant they leave my sight. Through security and onto the plane, I slip into a zombie-esque state, tranquilized with Ativan. The secret makes me sick to my stomach. Slammed by this sudden betrayal, by the disbelief that I am leaving my country, and everything I know, for the possibility of abandonment, my body feels lifeless. Sinking into my seat on the plane, I sob. I have no knowledge of Basel, the Swiss border town where I will land near nighttime, nor do I have any clue if Jean-François will be there when I arrive.

The flight attendants do not ask questions; they gently move me to a private block of empty seats in the back of the enormous plane. Likely, they have assumed someone beloved has died, because of my uncontrollable river of tears. Two bring extra blankets and pillows, suggesting I stretch out and, before the younger steward leaves, he looks kindly into my eyes, and gently squeezes my hand.

Gradually, I fall into a drug-induced sleep, while the effects of a second Ativan swirl through my system. My last thought is of arriving at an empty European airport.

THREE
FRANCE

Au Revoir

November / Novembre

This place where you are right now, God circled on a map for you.
—Hafiz

Departing the plane in a daze, I walk the long corridors without a single idea of what I will do if he is not there. When I spot Jean-François awaiting my flight with a bouquet of flowers and a strained smile, I am simultaneously awash in relief and anxiety.

With little conversation, we drive to an evening market in the small town he had described—our temporary residence—and the market is exactly as I'd imagined it would be. We are there to purchase whatever food I would like for the week.

"Ohhh ... so this is the lovely Canadian girl you bought the flowers for! It is so nice to finally meet you," says the smiling florist.

With arms outstretched, the hardy fishwife greets me.

"Ahhh! We have heard so much about you. Welcome. Do you like fish? Which of my fish would you like to take home for dinner tonight?" she asks, proudly turning the catch of the day to show its best side.

Warmly chattering, the cheese lady wraps some fresh, homemade wedges that I cannot identify, welcoming me to France.

These women know of me? He has spoken of me? Why this, then? What has happened to change things so quickly, without warning?

The weather is wet and cold and grey and, with our silence, the sound of the windshield wipers slapping in the drizzle is deafening. He takes me to an old stone house in the small town of Mulhouse.

When I ask whose it is, his only response is, "A friend's."

Without deliberation, I sleep in Jean-François' bed the way women have done for millennia, when dumbstruck by deception. But I am numb. All of the euphoric memories of lovemaking in Lisbon have evaporated. The soft, liquid pleasure I knew of this man has dissolved into a mist of bewilderment, my body hard and icy.

In the morning, I arise with him while he prepares for work. Over breakfast, he bizarrely fusses over how I butter my toast.

A newspaper with apartments for rent circled in red sits on the table. Recently, we had discussed renting a place in Mulhouse for my six-month leave; I would be in a town, rather than alone in the countryside, during any of his shorter *déplacements* of which I would not accompany him. He says we will look at the ads in the evening, and with no further fanfare, leaves for work.

Jetlagged and hung over from the Ativan, I slip back under the covers to sleep until mid-afternoon. The skies are black, and rain is coming down in cats and dogs when I awaken. I have no idea where I am, and the dismal weather only adds to my confusion; a cloud of angst hovers over me.

It is evening, and we are out at a small restaurant in a nearby town. With no tourists in this area, the owner of the restaurant is curious about me, and asks questions.

On our way back to the big stone house, Jean-François asks why I felt the need to speak to the man for so long, and is clearly jealous. He also asks about my hairband.

"Women here don't wear those," he states with absolute surety.

"Right now, I really don't care what women here wear. I wear hairbands."

"Well, in France, we do things differently."

The nerve of him.

All of my pent up hurt and confusion spews volcanically, my face hot in fury.

"You are an asshole!" I scream.

"You think I am azzz-ole?" he questions, looking at me, and then back at the dirt road.

"Yes. A first rate asshole. I do not understand this game you're playing. It's unbelievably cruel."

With my emotions cooled, back at the house we discuss the various apartments, but we do not go to visit any. Informing me that he must work in Leon on the weekend, he says I am welcome to go along. But things are clearly not well enough between us, and the tension is thick and mounting.

He asks what I will do in France while he is gone to India, and I tell him about the freelance writing ideas I have outlined in my project book. With my limited French, I am unable to properly explain my research, and he pish-poshes the idea.

"I still don't understand why you've taken this contract, Jean-François. We made clear plans. I agreed to come to France for at least six months; you agreed to stay in Europe for six months. There was no grey area."

Walking to a small credenza in the hallway, he picks up a thick document. He hands it to me to read but, of course, it is in French. His divorce decree has recently arrived, and it states that he will not only pay child support, but a substantial monthly alimony to his ex-wife.

Like men the world over, he is angry and disbelieving that he must pay something decided by a judge, based on law. Obviously, he believes it is unjust. The details of their break-up is not something we have discussed, so I don't know if it is fair or harsh. However, I doubt I would be given an impartial, two-sided story if I asked.

He waves the papers in the air, and says it is a lot of money, and that the contract in India is lucrative, one he needs to accept. Something in his demeanor leads me to wonder what she went through in this divorce. One temporary work contract will not change the course of this financial agreement. He knew to expect child support and should willingly pay it and, with French law, he had to have known he would be required to pay alimony. He understood this was coming; I don't accept it as an excuse for this drastic turn of events, this Jekyll and Hyde situation.

Lost in a fog of uncertainty all day, I'm still unsure of what is happening. Jean-François has come home from work, and tells me that all employees at his company have been mandated to learn English. The newly arrived American trainer desperately wants to meet me to ascertain if I would be a suitable assistant to help teach English to the large staff.

Voilà! A step in the right direction. Although I still feel wobbly and tentative with our broken agreement, I may have something to do for the time he will be away.

Traveling backwards once again, the tone has shifted today. Jean-François suggests I go back home to Canada and return to France after his contract in India is completed. Working with the English teacher has somehow been dismissed as an option, and I have the distinct feeling that it is due to his possessiveness.

He thinks this is a good plan; he appears to believe I should find it perfectly acceptable to pack up and go back to Canada—to what, I'm not sure—and return at a later date. At his convenience.

What have I done? What in the bloody hell have I done?

Treading water to maintain equilibrium, I strain to think clearly, but feel myself being sucked into an undertow that threatens to drown me. After all of our long calls and his many letters declaring love and undying commitment, this man clearly does not understand the breadth of the betrayal he is perpetrating. He seems not to grasp what it took for me to get here: the gut wrenching decision; the courage; the planning; the work—God—*the work*, to wrap up my life in Canada.

The honor he depicted has all but vanished. Had the situation been reversed, I would have done everything in my power to make his arrival into Canada one of comfort and safety. With an unquestionably warm welcome, he would have felt cherished and loved. I have received quite the opposite. His selfishness and blatant disregard for my feelings stings me to the core.

From out of clear blue absurdity, he comments on my anklet. Proper women don't wear them in France, he says.

What. The. Fuck?

Nothing in this scenario makes sense. Where is the charming, tender man I fell in love with? Where is the man who was so excited for my arrival, and spoke such endearing words of love to me less than two weeks ago? My heart feels like it has been ripped from my chest and thrown to the floor.

I sit down at the kitchen table, everything reconfiguring in my brain. I make a decision, incredulity stamping it with a seal of adamancy.

"If I go now, Jean-François, I go forever."

"*Mais non!* You can come back after Christmas, after this contract is over."

"*Non.* I am telling you, definitively, that if I leave now—if you let me go—I go forever. I will never return to France for you. It took everything I had to get here. I gave up my life to be with you. I have no car, no furniture, and no home. Someone else has filled my job for the next six months. I gave you my heart, without reservation. This is it. We either make this work now, or never. We find an apartment before India, or I leave. *Forever.*"

With rock solid certainty, I know that I will never return if I leave now. This was too big a risk, too monumental a move. I made my decision to come here without coercion, and I knew it had a fifty-fifty chance of success. But to be dismissed in such a manner, before any chance to discover whether our love will continue to grow, is unacceptable. To be sent off callously, with no consideration for what I have done to get here, is unconscionable.

Dawn's light peeks through the wooden slats, rousing me from a fitful sleep.

What happens to the body, to the cells, when up goes down overnight?

Facing away from Jean-François, I lie in bed contemplating this idea. That sweet can turn sour so swiftly is both sad and surreal.

He awakens and rolls toward me, I, instinctively recoiling. He blathers, still certain that his plan is a good one.

With no need to discuss it any further, I ask him to buy me a ticket to Paris before he goes to Léon. He wants to know why I want to go to Paris, but I refuse an explanation. He deserves none. Grabbing my robe from the bedpost, I climb out of the high bed, and reiterate that I need a ticket to Paris, *tout de suite*.

After breakfast, he agrees to make arrangements for a plane ticket today at his travel agency, smugly believing I will return soon. When he leaves, I repack the few things I have taken from my bags. The gifts and Christmas paraphernalia that I bought with such love and care for him and his son, the boy I have not yet met, he can ship back to my mother's house.

Thinking over the sequence of events of the past six months, I sit in disbelief at the window of the cold, stone house of unknown origin. After everything I have done to get here, I cannot fathom that I will be heading to Paris without a plan, in the most unexpected manner imaginable.

"Can I help you, Miss?"

"*Non. Non. Merci,*" I mumble, as tears stream down my face, pooling in the V that stops at my now soaked bra.

Sitting on my two preposterously heavy and cumbersome suitcases—the ones I thought I would be living out of for the next six months—I sob uncontrollably outside the metro station near the airport.

Leaving Jean-François at the airport in an abyss, I am paralyzed by confusion in this large, foreign city. Monique, my Canadian friend in Paris, was supposed to meet me upon my arrival; she has made the arrangements for my hotel, and I do not know where I am going next.

I spot a phone booth across the busy street, but I cannot carry my assortment of bags, and the two huge cases, another step. I cannot stop crying. People pass by, speaking a language I only moderately understand, the occasional person glancing over at my sorry display, but I am too distraught to be embarrassed.

Where is Monique?
Have I gotten off at the wrong stop?
Why am I in this city?

I do not know how long I have been sitting on this street, as I piece together the events of the past week and try to make sense of them, arranging them like a puzzle into something my mind can accept as valid. The same man who stopped earlier gently touches my shoulder.

"Miss," he says, in heavily accented English, an accent that I have come to adore. "You have been here for an hour like this. I cannot bear that you are still crying. I must help you. What can I do?"

Crawling out of my trance through the torrent of tears, I ask if he will carry my bags to the phone booth. Anxiously awaiting my call, Monique picks up on the first ring. She confirms that I have gotten off at the wrong stop. I choke out words through my grief-induced mania, trying to speak through the boulder in my throat.

I had no plans to come to the city of light—not right now anyway. I am supposed to be nestled in a small, quaint village, eating foreign food with my French lover. I am meant to be testing domestic life with a man—cohabitating, possibly considering marriage, potentially becoming a landed immigrant far away from my birthplace.

And now I am here, in a bitterly cold Paris, where the grey skies are as bleak as my shattered heart, where the rain soaks my already sodden spirits. I have been hit by a tidal wave of epic proportions, my entire life awash in the devastation. Torn bits and pieces of it float through my mind.

The aftermath is yet to come—I cannot see ahead of this moment.

Monique arrives and she is, as usual, lovely and serene—a sharp contrast to the tangled mess that I am. Calling her from Mulhouse, I asked that she help find me a place to stay. She lives in a small *pension* with a woman she has befriended, and I had hoped to get a room there, but they have no vacancies. Instead, she has booked me a five-night stay at a central hotel and, in the meantime, I will look for a less expensive option.

Taking the Metro to the hotel, we check in and drop my things inside the room, then go to dinner so that I can explain the fiasco that has just unfolded. Attempting to recount the events of the past week, I am at a loss to understand them myself.

Writing extensive and explicit letters to each other since she left for France, I have sent numerous narratives about Portugal and Jean-François, and of my decision to come to the country she fell in love with after her escape from a stifling marriage. Knowing the full scope of our love story, Monique is rendered speechless.

Jean-François had asked numerous times why I was going to Paris, but I did not wish to tell him that my dear friend was here. What I do, or why I do it, is no longer any of his bloody business.

It is another seedy, desolate day in Paris. This is not at all what I had imagined would be my first experience in 'gay Paris.' Walking the streets in the biting cold for something to occupy my body and mind, the grey buildings I pass by are a blur. I don't care what this city has to offer.

The world is black; it filters through a miasma of whatever chemicals and hormones flood a body in betrayal. I was in love—madly, deeply in love. Am I supposed to now not be in love? In the blink of an eye, am I to change the landscape of my heart, and cast out this man who has pervaded my every thought since I first laid eyes upon him?

I cannot go through this again so soon. It took all of my reserves just to breathe after my husband left. Only a couple of weeks afterwards, I began a new, demanding position, and was forced to put my best foot forward, in spite of my grief and disbelief. Recently recovered from the trauma of cancer, I had to reinvent my life as a single woman in an established social life filled with couples, and in a home that still held his energy. I do not know if I am strong enough to endure another colossal blow on the heels of two shattering events.

Following the hotel map to the address of a shabby little office near the Arc de Triumph that specializes in locating rooms, I find its walls filled with scraps of notes and numbers. I am able to secure a room in an *arrondissement* close to the center of the city.

A fifty-something woman in a red Chanel suit blows smoke rings at me at a small corner café on the Rue des Francs-Bourgeois. The Parisians smoke incessantly, while I suppress the urge to scream. I want to throw every noxiously billowing cigarette on every street, and each café of this city, into the Thames. The food is exquisite, but the thick, acrid smoke that hangs everywhere annihilates my enjoyment of it.

Meandering, I think about Monique's life in this city. Twelve years ago she was a client and that is how our friendship grew. She owned an old-fashioned stationery shop, one of the last of its kind. I sold a vast array of stationery products and, for such a small store, she did a significant volume of business. The attraction for her clientele seemed to be her charm and elegance, more so than the products she offered. I noticed many men coming in to buy things, and then linger to visit with her.

When we first met, she was married to a control freak of a man. They had amassed wealth during the marriage—which afforded Prada clothing and vacations on the French Riviera. She lacked for nothing, but increasingly felt like a canary imprisoned in a gilded cage. Plotting her departure from the marriage, she was slow and methodical; with such a man, one must not make sudden moves. Finally she left, but freedom came at the cost of leaving much of the wealth behind. For her, it was worth it.

Once liberated, she began doing things she had only previously dreamt about; she backpacked throughout Europe one summer with a young friend, and fell in love with the French countryside. Back at home, she made a plan to close up shop, rent out her space, and move to France. Next, she boldly called a goat farmer, whom she had briefly met in the small town of Ceret, to ask if he had any room for a boarder.

For ten months she lived with an eccentric, difficult man, and his herd of randy, rambunctious goats, and walked many kilometers into town to get groceries and whatnots. Once the novelty wore off, she made her way to Paris, and has lived here since. Her existence is one of exotic travel, fascinating friends, fine food and wine, and her French lover—an enchanting Parisian life.

With our rich, weekly correspondence since she arrived in Europe, sending each other handwritten letters, sometimes thirty pages in length, we have shared our lives without censorship. I had envisioned weekend visits to Paris to get to experience her life firsthand. Never had I imagined being here under such wretched circumstances.

Monique is busy with her French paramour, and so I wander the city alone. In no way do I blame her for not spending a lot time with me right now. She is sympathetic to my plight, but I am depressing company, and well aware of my hollowness. After sleeping with the enemy for so long, she has created a wonderful life here, and I need not further piss on her Parisian parade.

Freezing from the damp cold of my room, I ask if it is okay to warm by the fire in the main living room of the house where I am staying. Madame sits down and questions me about why I am in Paris.

A disheveled and heavyset woman, she has abandoned the French propensity for fashion and impeccability. She is a pill, and wears a perpetual scowl, but I have been alone for days on the streets of Paris with my tortured thoughts, and I need to purge myself of this bewilderment.

Madame speaks only French, and I don't know where the words come from, but I express myself fluidly in her mother tongue. She listens attentively while I tell her my story. I stop speaking, and she leans back in her chair, folds her thick arms, and pauses momentarily.

Like an unanticipated blow, she suddenly leans in and yells, "*You stupid, stupid girl!* How could you believe an idiot Frenchman? How could you sell your house and come to France for him? Are you a complete fool? I can't believe it! This is *incroyable*, this story."

Cowering as the words hammer me, I am far too fragile to retaliate. Unsteady, I get up from the table and run to my room, falling onto the small, hard bed to weep.

I have been staying in the basement, in a makeshift addition to the house. The acrimonious Madame refuses to turn up the heat, because of the cost, and tells me I must also pay extra for hot water. This dungeon of a room is miserable, but I cannot muster the motivation to search for another place to stay, and then move these bags.

For ever so long, I lie still. Kicking someone who is so blatantly down and distraught is evil. While obsessing over this thought, a plot for reprisal sparks. I have never been a vengeful person; I devoutly believe karma is a boomerang for any wrongs we do. But I'm not fully sane right now—hopefully a temporary state. Karma flits through my mind while I, in daftness, root through her large bathroom cabinet to take something from her as retribution; the utter pointlessness of this eludes me. I find a pair of butter-soft black leather gloves and put them in my room—what for I don't know.

At a small desk with a dim light in the corner of the room, I set out the blank art cards and the watercolors I have brought with me for the purpose of sending updates to friends. I know they will be expecting something shortly. I force myself to paint small, simplistic watercolors of the Eiffel Tower and a Frenchman in a beret. Pathetically, I write lies in each of the cards, brief messages about the splendor of France.

A thick fog has crept in and curled through the corridors of my mind. I cannot comprehend the turn of events. Staring at the wall, I burrow deeper into my disgrace.

The bitch is right. I am a stupid, stupid girl. How could I have given up my life for him? What kind of a fool does this? How did I end up in Paris, in this hellhole of a room, freezing to death, weaving bullshit tales to friends? How on Earth did I go from the dream of a lifetime come true to *this*—all in the blink of an eye?

Like my husband did, another man I love has casually discarded me, and watched me walk out of his life. It is as though all I think I am is not so.

Je suis malade.
Complètement malade.

What to do, and where to go, ceaselessly rolls through my head like a child's train stuck on a circular track. I adore Greece, but the islands are bitterly cold and windy in the winter, and most of the cafés and restaurants close during off-season. Italy is stellar, but too expensive for my limited budget. The U.K. holds absolutely no interest to me, with its dreariness and dour culture, and nor do any other neighboring countries here. I must make a plan to leave. Europe is abysmal right now, and I do not want to be here any longer. In the throes of a code-red heartbreak, Paris in winter is not the place for me. I must go someplace with sunshine, and warmth, and a caring culture. Unequivocally, I cannot go home; returning so soon to nothing, wearing this heavy cloak of humiliation in a long, gloomy winter, I know, would be the death of me.

Walking the city streets for hours, staring in shop windows, I see nothing. I have always wanted to come to Paris, but everything is flat and dull and without a pulse. I find the underground further depressing, so I avoid it. Nobody notices me, and the waiters are only marginally civil.

Monique's lover, a thriving abstract artist, is presenting at the Eiffel Tower in a prestigious art exhibition. Standing off to the side, I observe. I have heard much about this interesting man. He is older—much older than Monique. Animated, he speaks with passion, and has the furrowed face of an intellect. He is a retired neurophysicist of some renown, and I do not understand the success of his art. A mess of heavy lines and squares on large canvases, potential buyers appear to be taken with the work.

I am always mystified when someone switches from one successful career to instantly flourish in a completely unrelated field. It seems some people are destined to prosper, while others, no matter what they do, or how hard they try, are not.

Gradually, I make my way back to the *pension*. The tropical forest within has grown silent. The fragrant flowers have wilted, and their dazzling petals have dropped to the earth, scattered in disarray. The sweet fruit is now rotting: bruised and abandoned. The flora chokes with weeds, and the heart of my secret garden is withered and parched with the sudden drought. The color has drained from the world; black and white and shades of grey are all that remain.

Monique stands on a bustling street corner wearing a long camel-colored coat with a matching beret, looking beautiful and chic and every bit French. She takes me on a tour to keep my mind off Jean-François. Wandering down the Rue de Rivoli, we visit the Louvre, and then Notre Dame. I have been collecting crosses from each place I go, and I buy a small silver pendant at the church. We stop in small shops; I pick out an inexpensive cameo and a tam, purchasing mementos out of habit, even though there is no reason I should want to commemorate this experience.

Monique asks what my plans are over wine in a small corner bar. We agree it is most unfortunate that I have been aimlessly roaming Paris without any appreciation of where I am. At first it had not occurred to me, because I am so far away, but the idea of Mexico dashed into my mind last night as I lay reading under a thick layer of scratchy blankets, shivering. Twice now, I have been to Puerto Vallarta. It is sunny and cheerful and I liked it very much. In Acapulco, Mazatlan, Mexico City, and Vallarta I have had excellent experiences with the Mexican people.

I tell Monique that I will speak with my sister to have her arrange a ticket back to Canada—only to exchange my suitcases, filled with mostly winter clothing, for one with summer things—and then leave immediately for Mexico. I don't wish to see or speak to anyone, aside from whoever will organize a quick swap.

This scheme is an unbelievable modification to my illustrious plans of romance in the south of France. Every fiber of my being was onboard with our plans for a life together. Fully cognizant that it might not work out, I am still not easily assimilating a departure almost immediately after my arrival.

I am a leaf that has been torn from its tree, tossed by the wind, tumbling through the air without a clear destination.

FOUR
MEXICO

The Soul of the Sun

December / Diciembre

When a lovely flame dies, smoke gets in your eyes.
—Otto Harbac

THANK GOD FOR THE SUN. AFTER THE DULL, GREY PALLOR of both Paris and Vancouver, Mexico is a welcoming bright blue, warm and alive.

One foot in front of the other, I found a place to live in a small Mexican hotel on a hill where only the manager, a pretty doe-eyed girl, speaks bits of English. There are no drunken tourist revelers here, no big buffets, no pool polo. For the next five weeks, I am situated in an expansive apartment—the 'penthouse'—with a view of the ocean, and a massive patio filled with a lush assortment of plants. It is a simple hotel, but I am deeply grateful for the space. It will help absorb my grief.

Ever so patiently, my sister handled the painstaking flight arrangements for my exit from France to Canada, then onward to Mexico. My heart told me I needed sunshine to heal, and I already feel the wisdom of its message. With absolutely nothing to say to anyone, the fact that I know no one in this city is fine.

Like a spy on a clandestine mission, only one friend knew of the situation. My mother packed a suitcase full of summer things for the exchange at the airport on my one-hour layover. Had I seen her, I would have fallen apart, possibly never to be put back together again. She arranged for Lynnette to pick up the bags for the swap. During our momentary trade, she told me about a conversation my father had had with Jean-François' mother; he tried to enlist her help in this debacle, but she wanted nothing to do with it.

Avoiding my hometown, I flew to Vancouver for two nights and, as fate would have it, my sister booked a hotel in the neighborhood where my boss and his wife live. Feeling like a prisoner, I stayed near the hotel to ensure I did not run across them in a sickening irony.

Now settled in at Hotel Paloma del Mar, it is the start of December. The moderate weather agrees with my body, keeping it at a comfortable equilibrium, and the sun refuses to let me wallow in bed. I walk each day, wandering high into the hills, and up and down streets filled with fuchsia bougainvillea. I find Elizabeth Taylor and Richard Burton's homes, joined by a bridge. A clever idea: separate houses united, but even that did not help their love survive.

The children, the stray dogs, the cats, and the small birds in cages along my way, are all grateful for my unfettered attention. They ask no questions. I walk until I am exhausted, and I sit at the beach for soul-soothing sunsets; some blue-hued, some pink, others fiery red-orange. The sun works diligently to melt the cold, hard shell that envelops me. She flickers as she drops behind the mountain at the ocean's edge, ever trying to penetrate my gloom.

Well past midnight, I watch movies, the escape a temporary reprieve from my madness. After, in the shadowy silence, I cry.

The speed with which love goes from the color and luminosity of the sun's light to an oppressive, blue-black, is swift. It is shocking. Like a shrimp on the bed, my body curls into fetal position, trying to protect itself from something that has already happened. Blood cells recoil and weep salty tears as they pass through a splintered heart. Sleep—unconsciousness—is my best friend right now, the only relief from the incessant, drubbing pain inside my brain.

A homeless man wanders my cobblestone side street most days. Shoeless and unkempt, with a wild Yeti appearance, he is an unusual sight in the heart of affluent Vallarta. Head down, mumbling to himself, he frequently stares at his dusty toes, hardened and browned by the sun. The first mentally ill homeless man I have seen here, vendors at the taco stands ensure he never goes hungry.

Daily, we greet each other in acknowledgement, aware of the other's condition. With veneration, he stopped me last week, to offer up a neatly wrapped chocolate muffin he had just received. Today, he holds out a hand with assorted pesos, and places them in my palm.

"Please take these," he mutters in Spanish, genuflecting once again.

Even in his fragmented state, this man sees the broken-ness in me, and wants to help heal my hurt. He makes me feel humanity is still good. A hard lump in my throat and tears stinging my eyes, I gratefully accept his gift.

Mum writes to tell me the natives are restless—and suspicious. The girls have been calling to ask where I am, and why I have been so silent. As much as I adore romance, I am a woman's woman, and love my girlfriends to the edge of the Universe. But this abyss I stand at the edge of, eddying with shame and humiliation, has rendered the verbose me wordless. I cannot speak of it.

Lying in bed, I stare at an unimaginably tiny lizard licking the sweat off my water glass, and the memories of the troops that landed from everywhere, when I was in the midst of dealing with the diagnosis of breast cancer, flood my mind.

In their infinite compassion, the nurses whisked me off into a private corner room at the end of the ward. Not once, did anyone stop friends or family, no matter the hour—even on the night three *amigas* burst in near midnight bearing a basket filled with delectable food, complete with a red-checkered tablecloth, for a bed top picnic. Flowers crammed every nook and corner, and a formidable cloud of love descended upon me in that little hospital room. It kept me safe. Right now, alone in this little Mexican hotel far away, I nourish my shattered self by feeding off the knowledge that I am loved, somewhere.

Seemingly irrational, this loss has hit me harder than the diagnosis of cancer. A strong belief in my ability to conquer the disease, and an ardent will to stay on Earth, to do what I came here to do, gave me fortitude. Jean-François has rocked me to the core of my soul. He invaded my blood—my very being. Nothing has ever rendered me mute, yet this cataclysm has.

I want time to rewind. I want him to be the man he pretended to be, to love me the way he professed, to live the words of undying devotion he spoke of with such conviction.

I want him to un-break my heart.

The gravitational pull of sadness permeates the air around me. I know this, because strangers—Mexicans—stop me on the street to ask if there is anything they can do to help me. Only one power in the world can heal me right now, and I am too numb to pray for that help. Divinity deceived me. Angels aligned to orchestrate

Lisbon. They rushed in to heed my wish, and I walked into a dream. And then, they watched me plummet, falling headlong into Dante's Inferno.

I torment myself by listening to the French love songs that aided and abetted my falling in love with a Frenchman. Aching to once again feel the ecstasy that raced through my body in Lisbon, I feel only agony. Replaying events over and over, I am obsessed with the details, perseverating, expecting to find an answer in the songs. But of course, there are none.

Like a character in a Jane Austen novel wasting away from consumption after the betrayal of a lover, I lay lifelessly on the bed. At home, I would be given a bottle of Prozac to conceal and coat the sorrow, to hide it away from the world and carry on, fraudulently.

Alone here, with nobody's advice or opinions, I am permitted to process the grief—to feel it—not tuck it away, and add yet another thick layer to the crud of my already sullied psyche. I know that to gloss over this ache, and try to hide it under a façade, could be detrimental to my health. I know I must live it in order to release at least a part of it.

Dear Sister,

This is the first time I have ever heard you so defeated, and I understand. It's hard to be so far away, and still so close to your pain. I wish I could do more. But I know you need time to mend your wounds, and build your strength and spirit again. You sound like every cell in your body has been traumatized. I felt the same way after my accident; I only wanted to sleep my life away. But things will get better. Those cells will heal. The spirit will fight on. You are not a quitter—your soul will rebuild, and your spirit and zest for life will come back, my dear sis.

Allow yourself to feel the pain. Don't fight it, or think you have to be anything for anyone. You have no one there to expect anything of you, so that is good.

Please know that your life is not a joke, or jinxed, or doomed to be a constant battle. In order to truly love the sunshine, one must feel the rain.

I have always admired you. I love your passion for life, for risk-taking, your spunk, your ability to weather through the storms, and be the one who brings the sunny balloons with cheerful brightness, while others are grey and dull and have given up.

Don't give up.

It's okay to be there right now, so that you can heal— but don't change you—a beautiful you, a you that I have always wished I could be. Even though we are different in many ways, I have always secretly wanted to be more like you. And sometimes, I have stepped out and done that, but with you being the one who leads the way first. You have always been my example to follow, my truth teller, my rock to lean on, and my best friend. I love you to the moon, and don't want to see you harden that precious, playful soul. Please step out of yourself at some point to be the observer, and see that you are still you, and no one or nothing can take that away from you.

So life, therefore, is good, because you are so very unique and priceless and you can make it whatever you wish it to be.

All my love,
Your sister

Down the little hill from my hotel is a restaurant with food that is hearty and homemade, and like a much-needed hug. Family-owned, there is no pretense or pomp, and I feel comfortable in this rustic, open-air café. Tonight, Pepe, the owner, a huge man with a sweeping moustache, sits at my table.

"You have been coming in here a lot. We are worried about you. What has happened to make you so sad?"

I do not have the inclination to speak with anyone about my fall from grace, but he is determined, and will not leave until I say something, so I offer up a brief summation of why I am in Mexico.

"Do not worry! All of us at Casa de la Salsa are your family now. My sons, me, my waiters, we will all take care of you. *Mi casa es su casa.* You come in anytime, and we will be here for you. You understand?"

"Yes. *Gracias.*" I choke out my appreciation.

He means it with all of his heart, and his sincerity fills a corner of my emptiness. Tonight, I am a little less alone.

I stare at my feet, covered in a fine layer of dust from my street urchin's ambling. I miss the laughter so much. I want to frolic again. Why was I given a glimpse of Eden, only to have it ripped away? We so often lose our ability to identify what our version of play is as we grow older and life gets more serious, and we leave it behind as a long ago memory. Jean-François was childlike playfulness at its best.

In melancholic reverie for an indeterminate distance of space and time, it is with a Herculean effort that I rise from the edge of the bed and make my way into the bathroom. On a cracked clay tile near the toilet, a silver watch sits coiled. Dolphins flank each side of the face. It is a gift Jean-François sent me, before he knew that dolphins are one of my favorite things about planet Earth.

Tonight we have hot water, so I stand in stillness under the light cascade, hoping to be cleansed, wanting to wash away the residue of his touch on my skin.

Coercing myself into the kitchen, I make a large salad for dinner, and lay down to read afterwards. Awake into the wee hours of the night, I watch *The English Patient*. The movie is odd and disturbing and it cracks open the fractures inside of me. When the movie closes its credits, I begin to write. Poems. Words gush and bleed all over the bed ...

You don't have the right.
You lust,
then spill waterfalls of I love you's
covering everything in a mist of illusion.

You have only seen the shoreline of my ocean;
my storms are short, but tempestuous,
yet my lust does not wane.

I bruise, disappointingly frail and fragile,
but my lavender kisses will not die.

You will fear my appetites,
and my insolence is innate,
but when I dream,
the world is my smiling oyster.

My feline capacity for self-indulgence may incense you,
and the depth of the lake that holds my tears is unknown,
but when watered,
    my love yields incandescent blossoms of every color.

After you have sailed these waters,
and time has told on you,
only then
    is the privilege
      yours.

The Festival of Guadalupe is a Mexican celebration to honor the birth of the Virgin of Guadalupe, beginning on the 1st of December and culminating on the 12th. Women assemble small stands on side streets, and in the church plaza, to sell their finest cooking and baking; it is the best place to eat before Christmas.

I make my way out tonight to partake in the festivities, but in actuality, I am only an observer. Sitting on a crowded bench with a chicken *tamale* Oaxaqueño, I unwrap the oily banana leaf to reveal a large pocket of savory *maseca* stuffed with shredded chicken that is drenched in a dark mole sauce. The hot corn meal is comforting and earthy.

Children dressed immaculately in colorful indigenous costumes revel in this festival, a time for cake and cotton candy. Running freely through the square, they squeal and play games, chasing each other.

Melodically drifting down the streets in the distance, the anthem, *Guadalupana*, is sung repetitively in ritual, as the many pilgrims make their way around the street corner to the picturesque central church named for the Virgin. Couples snuggle next to each other at tables in the surrounding makeshift cafés, sharing tacos and tostadas and big bowls of steaming *pozole* soup.

The Mexicans' deep belief in the miracles of their 'mother'—their celebration of faith—caresses my childhood Catholic roots, but when I reach inside, I cannot find any residual devotion. The void is resounding.

I have fallen out of love with myself, swiftly, harshly. This is the greatest loss of all. Self-trust has become eroded and has all but vanished. It is one thing to be betrayed by a lover, but add to that the suspicion that you have deceived yourself, and the world becomes a landmine. If I cannot trust myself, whom and what can I trust?

I order a cold glass of *agua de Jamaica*, deep purple from the hibiscus petals, and leave the plaza to slowly walk the seaside *malecón*, back to my little hotel. The waves are high tonight, the moon full.

I do not want to admit to my bitterness and faithlessness, especially after watching the Mexicans celebrate in such a reverent and joyous manner. I want to believe I can go through this experience with grace, but I am jaded, and the murky acid festering inside is contaminating the part of me that forever believes—maybe like a fool—in true love, in my dreams.

Olivia stops me and hands me a fax that is sitting on the front desk. It is from my dear friend Robert. He has heard, via the grapevine, what has happened. He wants me to know that it's no big deal, it was an adventure, and I can move on.

Unable to control myself, I reply with a fiery missive that lumps him together with all of the bastards of the world. *Liars*, is what springs to my mind, all of them liars, telling me the sun rises and sets on my ass, declaring that they would move mountains to be with me, that they love me madly, deeply, truly.

The fax has been sent—too late to retrieve—and now that I

am back in my room, I already regret sending off my angry words so hastily. Our relationship came to a bittersweet end last year, but my note was most unfair.

Robert and I met at a trade show, while working across from each other for a week of torture, in a frozen prairie city with scavenging government workers seeking freebies every day. A jokester, he always had a hilarious remark about the vultures passing through. He kept me in stitches each day, and entertained our large group in the evenings at the tiny Italian joint we frequented, the good food our only solace in that godforsaken, ice-encased city.

By the final day, he and I were clearly lust-stricken. Since we traveled in the same circles to the same places, we knew we would have the opportunity to see each other again.

He was my après-divorce man. Immediately, we began having long phone conversations, plotting out our road trips to coincide.

Prior to Robert, I had really only known rogues. He was steadfast and sweet. As we grew to know each other, our fondness flourished. He was my first experience of being truly adored, head-to-toe. Nothing escaped his notice; every small detail, and each nuance about me—a new shade of lipstick or a light tan, a fresh pedicure or a three-pound weight loss—was acknowledged.

Catching on quickly to my hypoglycemic tendencies, he began to carry a cooler filled with savory snacks and icy piccolos of sparkling Cordo Negro (my drink du jour), for post-workday, pre-dinner 'decompression' time together.

Indulging my addiction to magazines, he would show up with the latest editions of my favorites, along with small, well-thought-out gifts. In turn, I would cook lavish meals when he was in my hometown, and pander to his penchant for pretty lingerie. Indulging each other, our liaisons were love-affirming 'givefests.' I found great satisfaction being in a relationship with a man who understood the fine art of giving and receiving.

In spite of it all, I knew that his innately domestic nature, and my wild-child ways, would not bode well for a long-term relationship. Only temporarily enamored, my semi-Bohemian lifestyle was exciting compared to his weekends of yard maintenance and childrearing.

Besides, he was on loan. Due to what he had perceived as a bold betrayal, he and his wife had separated. Also, he had recently lost his mother, a workaholic surgeon with a big presence in the community, and he was grieving profoundly, even though he was not aware of it.

Later, when he declared unending love, and announced his decision to move to my city to be with me, I had to make a hard choice. Selfishly, I would have reveled in having him for my own, basking in the attention and affection of a man such as he was. For a long moment, I entertained the notion. But in the end, my heart directed me to do what was right.

I told him what I foresaw: the first short while would be like a play-filled honeymoon. After a time, the daily phone calls that would surely come from his two little girls, begging him to come back, would flood him with unspoken guilt; he was not just a good dad, he was a phenomenal father, and I knew his judgment was momentarily skewed by a lopsided view of life with me.

His arrival would not herald an overnight change in my night owl behavior, European-style dining hours, and my habit of wandering off with girlfriends for endless periods. These would become a source of irritation and loneliness, and he would resent having turned his life upside down for me.

Eventually, if he decided to return to his wife, she would never forget—and likely never forgive him—for the time he ran away from his life to live with another woman. It would be a sticking point in any argument. I warned him that it would be a decision he would regret, and one that would be extremely hard to mend. He'd never spoken ill of her, and I knew that, deep in his heart, he still loved her. They could repair the damage and rekindle their stale relationship. With a tangled heart, I told him to go back to her and work things out. For months, he disagreed and argued his love for me. But ultimately, he saw the wisdom in my logic.

In reflection, I understand that we came together to heal, and to make the other a better person. With me, he lost weight, and stopped nervously chewing his nails to the quick. A workaholic, he learned how to relax, and discovered how to have fun again. I knew he left me with a different perspective toward making time for his family, and also a renewed appreciation for the preciousness of pleasure.

He primed me to love again, and opened my heart with a tenderness I had never known before. With him, not only did I blossom—in all ways—with the watering of his devotion, I acquired a new sense of self, and was confident in my skin in a changed way. Out on my own in the world again, I was willing to love and to be vulnerable. Given that he only showed adoration toward me, I hope he can forgive my harsh words.

A lonely week has passed. I stand on the patio, gazing at the moon glowing over utopia. Inside, I fall down on the bed and write.

A full blue moon over the castillo the last night of our foreign love
"Think of me always on a full moon"
and now I fear it will remain so
every month
of my life

Blackness stirring within once again, I furiously scribble a letter to Jean-François. I must spew and release this venom.

> *I hate you. I want to hurt you as much as you have hurt me. I want to discredit you with your family—anyone in your life. I want to destroy you as you have destroyed me ...*

I hurl invectives aloud at the walls and weep.
Later, my words morph on the page.

> *I love you. I ache for you in the middle of the night. I miss the sound of your voice. I wish you were here with me. I cry for you without end.*

I stumbled upon Cuizas, an inordinately exquisite restaurant on the Rio Cuale. Hidden from view is a large, lush patio filled with flowers, palm trees, and small lizards that dart about. At night, countless colorful hand-blown glass bowls filled with candles twinkle on the tiled bar and throughout the greenery, turning the place into a glittering dream.

The waiters are attractive and attentive, but Kevin, the manager, is especially engaging. Our conversations are warm, and I enjoy his manner. On past visits, we have discussed his business dreams for his new life in Mexico. Today, he appears somewhat tense as he sits down.

"You've been coming here a lot, and I really enjoy our conversations. But Wanda ... um ... I need to tell you that I *am* gay."

I laugh loudly. "Kevin. I am well aware of that fact. I have been coming here mostly because of you, but not because I had any romantic delusions."

A smile breaks, and his body slackens. Embracing me in a strong hug, he says he is happy that he can now talk freely. In a torrent, he tells me of his lover, and his life here in Puerto Vallarta. As he confides his secrets and bold plans, our friendship blooms. He is a luminous soul in my dark night.

In my delirium, the room swirls. I can barely lift an arm. I have been violently expelling from both ends, for what is likely only thirty-six hours, but feels like a year.

Earlier, the maid came in to clean, looked at me, and quickly found Adriana, who in turn called the doctor. It appears that I have amoebic dysentery, and he gave me a shot with potent pharmaceuticals, to kill it before it kills me. Thank God for a society with doctors who still make house calls.

Not helping my cause tonight, the *posadas* have begun in earnest. Raucous Christmas parties, they continue on throughout the night until dawn, and it seems the hotel is hosting every neighborhood party in the restaurant, one floor below. The blaring *banda* music—with its traditional, ear piercing yipping and howling—is not going to end anytime soon. I need a pair of earplugs, although there is no way to block out the pounding bass that rattles the frames of my doors.

Pleading into the emptiness, I beg for relief from the roiling agony. I am no stranger to physical pain. Only a short time ago, après cancer, I dragged myself to emergency, in a hospital where two of my friends nurse, at the end of an excruciating week. Lynnette quickly found the resident neurosurgeon.

For many months I had been in unrelenting misery, always

in search of a place to lie down, for any brief reprieve from the twisting pain in my back, which radiated down my leg, numbing my foot. In between sales calls, I would recline the seat of my car for a few minutes, before making the next visit. Tears were my constant companion, and I was on a garden variety of painkillers and anti-inflammatories. By the time I got to the emergency room on a Friday, I was walking laboriously, with knife-searing pain, dragging my right leg. I understood the elderly all too intimately, and I was at the end of my endurance.

With certainty, I explained to the resident, if he did not help me, I would either find heroin on the streets, or jump off the High Level Bridge. I meant it.

Pulling the CT scans of my spine, ones that an orthopedic surgeon had done months earlier at the hospital, he gasped, and scheduled me in for emergency surgery that Monday.

Secretly assuming that I was faking the pain for attention, the prickish head surgeon apologized directly after surgery. Scratching his head, he explained that he'd never seen someone so young—especially a female—with a disc that had completely 'exploded,' and was pressing so severely on the spinal cord.

What is planet Earth? A fucked up school of pain? Is it a place the unfortunately chosen of us come to experience a merciless spectrum of physical ailments that brings us to our knees, and emotional pain that rips our brains apart? Are carrots of joy dangled in front of us just to keep us moving forward in false hope, and then sadistically torn away for someone's amusement? Is this a sick game?

This dense, barbaric planet cannot be all there is. Whatever this reality or illusion, I want a new plan. I feel like a fish that has been cut open and gutted. I want out of this contract. I don't know why I agreed to come here, but I want emancipation.

Even though I need aid, I cannot, and will not, pray. My fractured heart refuses to speak.

A row of dominoes in front of me, I sit with two teenage boys who attentively play the game. I came for hot, homemade soup, something to ease me back into food since the despicable purge. Pepe's boys are sweet to entertain me; however, ageism is not a factor here. People of every age mingle at all manner of events, and it is not the youth who rule. Everyone is respected, and considered a valuable part of the whole, as it should be.

Never overly fond of games, I am still grateful for the diversion. Pepe's sons and his waiters have taught me an assortment of such since I arrived. In sincerity, they have taken on the task of helping me heal my heartbreak.

I leave Casa de la Salsa, filled with medicine, both for my belly, and for my spirit.

Jaime, a pleasant man who works at a place I pass by each day, has relentlessly asked me out. Twice I agreed to coffee, and he was good company. He has invited me to Guadalajara to spend Christmas with his family, and thinks it is absurd for me to be alone for the holidays.

The central square in Pitillal pulsates with traditional music, and is a kaleidoscope of color: pomegranate and sienna, terra cotta and sapphire, emerald green and ocean blue. Children race about with toy windmills and chase each other through the gazebo while *abuelas* watch with pride.

Jaime and I are enjoying the Sunday festivities and attending Christmas mass near the *barrio* where he lives. Worshippers have purchased their tiny *milagros*—small trinkets of everything imaginable: arms, legs, dogs, houses, babies—all representative of their needs or wishes, the miracles they petition for. They will pin them onto the dress of the Virgin of Guadalupe, a deity who has granted tens of thousands of such miracles in this country. Jesus hangs in sorrow above the altar, and the prayers of the Mexicans twinkle brightly in the neat rows of candles lit before the Tabernacle.

As the priest speaks, and the celestial music is sung, I stiffen in an attempt to suppress my tears, but in a church—especially when steeped in low spirits—I cannot. I am a fallen Catholic, yet these rituals and ceremonies are embedded in my cells. I don't believe the bogus rules, and manmade dogma, and misinterpretations of the bible, but this is where I learned of God. Even though I do not understand the homily, the ceremony is moving. Silently, I cry.

"Who are you trying to impress with tears?" Jaime asks when we leave.

Asshole.

Why take me to church? Who is *he* trying to impress?

I tell him it is pointless to keep asking me out. I don't want a loquacious Latin lover, nor do I want him to expect anything from me, or analyze me, as he has already begun to do. He asks too many questions that he has no business knowing the answers to.

Returning to my room, I drop onto the bed. Why do we yearn for comfort from the one who has hurt us so deeply? Why is it that we want the very man who has caused us such pain to wrap his arms around us, kiss our hair gently, and make it all go away? It is a most strange paradox of the female psyche—maybe the human psyche. I do not understand men whatsoever, so I cannot speak for them.

I spot a fax on the corner of the bed, one that the front desk has left in an envelope. It is from Monique. I remain curled on my side, and tear it open.

Ma Chère Wanda,

> *It seems like such a long time since you've left. Daily, I look for news from you. Voilà! Today, finally a letter has arrived.*

> *I re-read your letter; you are still in shock and deep pain. It's going to take time, Wanda. Be patient with yourself. It is good that you have found a decent place to stay, and the temperature sounds wonderful. You have the sand and the surf. Now relax, meditate—rest your mind to ease the pain and eliminate the anger.*

> *You will surely hear from Jean-François, for I am certain he couldn't have won over everyone if he were that insincere. He made genuine overtures to your family. You did not misjudge; no one could fault you for putting your heart and soul into this commitment. It failed, for only God knows what reason. But I know it is hard to make sense of this situation.*

> *Je t'embrasse,*
> *Monique*

Today is my birthday. Never had I imagined, especially this year of all years, that I would be spending it alone—in Mexico, no less. I had dreamed of a festive French birthday with my lover, eating croissants in bed *après faire l'amour* in the morning, lunch in the village, and dinner somewhere in the countryside. I can pretend that this is just another day and ignore my birthday, or

I can pull myself together, take out one of my pretty dresses, and honor today, in spite of this disaster.

Procrastinating, I sit on the edge of the bed, and watch an old sitcom to its boring end. A horrible documentary of World War II interrupts my indecision, and I abruptly shut off the television. One thing that baffles me to the core about this planet is war.

Birthdays are meant to be celebrated.

I select a gauzy periwinkle-blue dress—one that I retrieved in the suitcase exchange—romantic and flowing and chosen especially for European spring nights. I will go to Cuizas where I know the waiters will fuss when they find out it is my birthday.

As I maneuver my way down the cobblestone street in heels, I notice that Eduardo is working tonight at Casa de la Salsa. He is a cheery, warm man, generous with smiles and compliments. Popping in to say hello, I spontaneously ask him out.

"Eduardo, it's my birthday today."

He hugs me and wishes me a heartfelt *feliz cumpleaños.*

"I am going to Cuizas for dinner, and I was wondering if, after your shift, you would be so kind as to go dancing with me?"

"*Claro que sí!* Of course I will go! I would love to take you dancing. I will be off before midnight."

"Okay. I will come back for a drink, and then we shall go dancing. *Gracias* Eduardo."

"No! *Gracias á ti!* See you later."

The host seats me at a small table surrounded by purple bougainvillea flowers and palm fronds on the garden patio near the edge of the river at Cuizas. Tonight, the gorgeous, green-eyed Adan is my waiter. As usual, Kevin's restaurant is immaculate, with candles twinkling in every corner and nook. I am about to tell Adan that it is my birthday, when a flock of handsome waiters surround me to say hello, and a glass of Chardonnay is placed in front of me, before I have asked for one.

A bored woman in a floral caftan, sitting with her further disinterested husband, watches the flurry of waiters bring a salad, then an appetizer, and next my main course, all the while loitering about to chat me up. Another large group is also closely observing the activity, and I feel my face redden; I will not mention my birthday after all. It would be too much of a scene for a woman alone.

Dining out solo at a young age, because of my business life on the road, I am usually comfortable. Still, eating alone in a foreign country can be intimidating. One night in Greece, I ate at a quaint outdoor café on the island of Mykonos. A sharply dressed older woman, accompanied by a distinguished gentleman, watched me as though I was a roadside attraction. I got indigestion and left quickly. My assumption was that she was judging me, or feeling sorry for me, but I later realized that she could well have been admiring me for my bravado.

With a flourish, Adan presents a thick slice of rich *tres leche*s cake, on the house, which I can only make a marginal dent in. I feel overfed when I finally take leave to walk back to Casa de la Salsa.

Strolling the *malecón* is always an event, in and of itself. Building a mini Stonehenge using the laws of physics, a man glistens with sweat as he heaves humongous stones, and tries to find the point of balance. A most odd way to make a living, but inventive.

The tempo is picking up for Christmas, and three buskers sing along the way; one an American classic, one an old Spanish folksong, the other a sad Mana song about a woman who stands on a pier each day awaiting her lover, a man who swore he'd return to her, but never does.

Sola, sola en el olvido ... Alone, alone in oblivion.
Sola con su espíritu ... Alone with her spirit.
Sola ... Alone.

Sitting at the bar for a margarita, I chat with Pepe and his sons while I wait for Eduardo. The restaurant is slow tonight, so he is able to leave earlier. We head to The Zoo, a loud, popular club on the *malecón*.

Eduardo is attentive, and has the DJ dedicate *Las Mañanitas* to me, the much better Mexican version of Happy Birthday. The bartender garnishes my cocktail with fresh flowers and two colorful umbrellas, and gives me a birthday kiss on the cheek. All thoughts of doom are chased away with their kindness.

Dancing our way into the small hours of the morning, Eduardo walks me back to my hotel as the sun begins to rise over the Sierra Madres.

I am proud of myself for finding the courage to go out for my birthday, instead of giving in to the call of the wallow. Exhausted, I fall into a restful, dreamless sleep.

Hello my friends,

It is with tremendous difficulty that I write this letter. I have been attempting a self-imposed exile—incommunicado—and the notion still appeals to me. But it would seem a little odd, wouldn't it? After all of our shared excitement. After all of your help and support in my preparations for a new life in France. After you, my friends, sent me off in style, with so much love.

What am I doing in Mexico, you ask? This question, I ask myself ten times a day.

At this particular moment, I very much wish my

personality were more one of quiet discretion. I have shouted from the mountaintop to all: my friends, my acquaintances, my customers, my relatives—anyone interested in listening to my unbridled enthusiasm for my love story. And this is now what breaks me.

You have all seen me through one disaster to another. You've patiently given your TLC through my many maladies, and spent hours supporting me through my heartbreaks. But this is the final humiliation.

Not because of your reactions—you've come to expect the unexpected with an open mind and giving heart. It is your family and friends, and all of the people I've told—it is these people's opinions that I cannot bear. All of the "I knew it wouldn't work" or "that was a stupid thing to do" or "what did she expect?" or "how long did she know him?" and on it goes. These people don't know me; they don't know the circumstances, and the deliberation it took for me to take such a bold chance. I ask, as a favor, with all my heart, that you please not discuss this with the world at large. The thought of people either pitying me, or declaring me a fool, is too much negative energy.

What happened? To tell the truth, I myself am in a daze of uncertainty. Jean-François had been given a lucrative posting in India. This, and apparently financial issues in regard to his divorce, caused my departure. He thought it best I return to Canada, and come back sometime after Christmas. The enormity of the risk I took to move there seems to have eluded him for reasons I cannot comprehend; legitimate stress, unabashed lying, or insanity? I don't know.

I flew to Paris in a state of shock, and stayed there

for a short while to collect myself (which I still have not been able to do). Since I have no home to go to, so to speak, I came to Mexico to rehabilitate and rest. Paris was too expensive, too cold, and too unfriendly. I have an apartment in a small Mexican hotel off the beaten path.

My plan is to stay for the balance of my leave of absence from work, although my plans don't appear to be in my hands.

I trust the fog will lift. At least it always has before.
Love,
W

The shrill ring of the bedside phone jolts me out of the pages of my book. Loud music blares on the line, and Susan is on the other end, clearly inebriated. She is taking care of my territory, and staying in my business apartment for six months. She also purchased my new car in my life's sell-off.

My career in sales was not a well thought out decision; it was a choice made by a restless young woman fleeing the confines of a difficult home life at only seventeen. With a promoting-style personality and a natural sales instinct, it seemed like the obvious option. Unfortunately, the average sales manager is untrained in how to manage human beings. Most lack common sense, and are rife with insecurities and paranoia. Thankfully, the man who owns the company I now work for is the most wise and level-headed person I have known; he is a breath of sanity in a world of mostly drones. At my interview, I knew that I had found a real human being—a bona fide 'soul boss'—someone who worked on instinct and intuition, instead of pointless protocols and egoist rollercoasters.

There is nothing like the feeling of someone who gets you, and implicitly understands your value. Ron is that someone. After my first year with the company, I was given an unprecedented raise, in part because he considers me his only 'no-maintenance' rep. The better he treats me, the more loyal and hardworking I am. What the typical manager doesn't understand about this simple equation boggles the mind. Not only is Ron a fair and intelligent man, he is fun to work with. He shares my love of gourmet food, and the need to eat in a timely manner (no stopping at Subway, on the run, for this man). A master of human nature, with a great sense of humor and a balanced lifestyle, he doesn't expect ridiculous hours from anyone.

"It's our Christmas party," Susan yells, on the other end of the line. "Brad insisted on calling you! I didn't know what to say. You have to pretend you're in France ... he's coming ..."

My head explodes, and my face burns hot and red. Freezing in blankness, my brain feels like a malfunctioning computer, and I have no idea what I will say. I hate lying. Ron's son is on the phone, boisterously asking what time it is in France. I look at the clock, and frantically take a guess at the time conversion. He asks about France and Jean-François, and I lie, and then lie some more, and I feel like an utter asshole.

Susan is back on the line, and informs me that she has used Brad's credit card to make the call.

Jesus Cristo.

Before the bill comes in I will have to confess to the embarrassing truth.

I discovered a tiny, bustling salon owned by a pretty, young, pregnant woman, lush and mango-ripe, and being pursued by a young man who is not the father.

Gina is my manicurist. She's got attitude with a capital A, a girl from California with a combination of street smarts and degreed intelligence. Visiting Vallarta on a vacation a few years ago, she instantly knew that this was her home. Leaving behind a career working with juvenile delinquents as a social worker, she trained as a nail technician.

A Latina with a blend of Italian, Peruvian, and Venezuelan blood, she speaks both perfect English and Spanish. She's a bedazzling beauty, with cascading curls that reach almost to her waist, large brown eyes, and stunning bone structure: if she knows it, she doesn't show it.

Gina is friendly in an odd way; she scares me a little with her smartass demeanor (it reminds me of the tough chicks in high school who used to torment me), yet, underneath the façade, I feel the energy of a good heart. She bobs and weaves her head when making a particularly opinionated point—a Californianism. She asks a lot of questions, but it feels good to talk to another woman, to unburden a little. With the mark of a true artist, she has painted my nails with detailed designs, free hand, and I know I will come back to see her again.

Days have drifted by without account. An old Mexican man reads tarot cards in a corner at Una Página en el Sol, the main bookstore and café, chock-full of used and reused books. This place is a favorite of the ex-pats who loiter for hours, reading and visiting.

Hoping for good news, I ask the old man for a reading. With cappuccinos in hand, he accurately tells me about my situation, my character, my weaknesses and strengths. He offers no miracles in my near future, but he is wise, and his gentle eyes are comforting.

I stock up on another supply of novels, which I devour nightly. They keep my mind occupied when I am alone, and allow me to escape into other worlds made from the imagination of other people.

A friend, Delores, had been calling since my letter of confession, and wanted to come to Mexico for Christmas. In no shape for company, I advised her that I would not be a suitable holiday companion. I am fully aware of what I am right now; I cannot entertain anyone. I told her that I preferred she not empty her pockets and come all this way to spend the holiday season with a sooky-faced friend. She insisted, indicating that she understood and would not expect anything of me; she wanted only to ensure I am all right.

She arrived yesterday, true to her word that she wanted to check on me. She came armed with a care package from my sisterhood of friends; their love and care astounded me to tears.

My heart is set—in stone—on a traditional turkey dinner for today, Christmas day. I painstakingly searched the city, and found a three-course dinner at an old hotel, Agua de Molinas. It is one solid, 'normal' thing that I want for Christmas, and we are booked for the last seating of the day.

Down the *malecón* and over the bridge in the late afternoon sun, we walk to dinner. Ordering drinks, I salivate in anticipation. Our waiter smiles and informs us that, unfortunately, they have run out of turkey. He shrugs as I glare at him with incredulity.

Heat rises from my gut. An irrational anger erupts out of the center of my body, and I explode uncontrollably.

"I booked this well in advance. You have reservations for turkey dinner, so you should have planned accordingly. I want you to go back into that kitchen, and find two turkey dinners. I came for turkey, and I am getting turkey. *With* cranberries. If you don't have any in that kitchen, you'd better find it elsewhere!"

Delores is pink with embarrassment, but I continue to fume, unconcerned about my outburst. I want the fucking turkey. That's all I care about right now. I want *one fucking thing* to work out the way I planned.

Five minutes later, the waiter comes back with the dregs from the bottom of the pan—not great, but enough scraped together to make two meals. I eat in silence, comforted by the hot gravy, the sweet berries, and the home-centric food that soothes a ravaged and upside down part of me.

With comic relief, a letter arrives, via fax, from my baby brother.

From: El Cheapo Grande, New Zealand
Christmas Day, December 25th, 1996, 9:17 a.m.

Alrighty then! So, you're in Mexico now. Does this mean you're a fugitive? The French are idiots anyway (not all of them, of course). It's not a good time to be in Paris. The heat of Mexico will keep you preoccupied trying to find shade and a cool drink, and not reflecting on how your life is in a state of uncertainty, disarray, and the holyshitness of enough already.

So, how is life in the fast lane? Were you so envious of my hobo lifestyle that you decided to give it a go? Perhaps the difference between you and me is that I jumped into it head first, and you were kind of nudged off the cliff. Oh well, welcome to the world of rainbow warriors. How do you like it?

I spoke to our sister this morning, and she tells me you're thrilled with your new miserly living arrangements. Cool, eh? Just let me know if you need any pointers.

What will you do next? Are you going to wait around in Mexico for a while? It's nice that Delores was able to go down to spend Christmas with you. She's got a good heart. It seems Christmas will be unusual for all of us this year. Yesterday was the first time I mowed the lawn on Christmas Eve. It gives new meaning to the song, 'I'm Dreaming of a White Christmas'. I hope this will not turn you off Mexico. How does the song go? "Blue Spanish Eyes ... teardrops keep falling down from Mexico ..."

Love,
Your bro.

One day past Christmas, Olivia stops me as Delores and I walk out of the lobby. A call has just come in. I pick up the phone on the front desk and, with the sound of his voice, my heart stops beating. Blood fills my head, and the pounding blocks out the sounds of Mexico. It is Jean-François.

"How did you find me?" I ask in French. In a confusing mélange, my brain floods with both fury and elation.

"I called your sister and asked her where you were. I begged her for the number. What are you doing in *Mexique*?" he says.

"It's none of your business what I'm doing here."

"Are you working there?"

"No."

"Are you with another man."

Hmmmph, I huff through pursed lips.

"No."

"Come back. I have the apartment. Everything is fine now. Please come back to France," he whispers seductively.

"Are you *crazy?*"

"*Mais non!* Come back. I will explain later."

Volleying back and forth on this tangent, not once does he ask how I am doing. The phone crackles, and the connection is lost.

I walk out of the lobby door and down the steep, broken steps onto the cobblestone street, disoriented. Tears sting my eyes, and a cold wave runs through my veins with the realization that he did not even think to come here to get me. I shiver in spite of the heat.

After all I did to get to France, it does not occur to him to get on a plane to mend things, for him to make the effort this time instead of me. He thinks I should pack up my things, collect my broken heart off the streets of Vallarta, and arrange a flight out of Mexico to return to France. It is pusillanimity.

I am swallowed back into the pit of blackness that I have only marginally begun to dilute.

Delores is doing her best to keep my mind off the call, and onto the moment and the pleasures of this tropical sanctuary. Deeply grateful for the diversion, she helps to keep me from digressing back into an utter wretch.

It is New Year's Eve, and we have planned an evening out at a pretty restaurant with an ocean view and a special menu. Thankfully, I had enough wits about me to ask my mum to pack a little black dress. Fortuitously, we have been seated at a small table on one of the few patios facing the ocean, and the atmosphere is festive. Drinking margaritas and dining on a delectable meal, the evening is picture-perfect, with a warm sea breeze, crashing waves, and live music. Our waiter flirts and teases relentlessly, convincing Delores to try her hand at Spanish lessons.

A large group of Americans celebrate raucously, and one tall man with a self-assured aura comes over to our table. He invites us to join them for a bottle of Dom Perignon. Squeezing in, they welcome us with two glasses of icy champagne and trays of tapas. The tall man has just purchased the football stadium in Chicago, and this is his victory night. Everyone is in high spirits, and the champagne is giving both Delores and I a case of the giggles.

We bid farewell and make our way down the *malecón* to La Dolce Vita to celebrate the rest of the night away with the tribe of sexy Italian and Mexican waiters who have included us as guests at their private after-hours party. A deliriously happy Delores stops along the way to offer New Year's Eve kisses to an assortment of more than willing men.

In full-blown party mode when we arrive, we are whisked upstairs to a premium ocean view table. Martino, a dark and steamy waiter, takes me to the balcony to view the fireworks that have begun, and gives me a warm hug and a light kiss on the cheek. Frequently dining at the bar alone, I have become well known to the staff.

Dancing and laughing the night away, the festive evening ends as day breaks, Delores and I taking leave to tipsily meander down the streets of Mexico. I drop off to sleep, all thoughts of France washed away by champagne and the revelry of a wild Vallartan night.

January / Enero

The cure for anything is saltwater—sweat, tears, or the sea.
—Isak Dinesen

UPON MY ARRIVAL HERE, ALL THE SPANISH I HAD PREVIOUSLY learned eluded me. Sifting through the foreign language files of my mind, French sprang from my mouth in response to the Mexicans. Now, my brain has reversed; the trauma has caused me to abandon all words associated with Jean-François, and the little Spanish I know is coming back to me. Arriving at the hotel, I ask Olivia my question of the day, *"Hay algún recados?"* (Are there any messages?)

Long faxes filled with news and encouragement come in weekly from my sister. Today, a care package has arrived. She has mailed a variety of treats, and a creamy avocado-colored shirt, perfect for the temperature right now. Still wandering around 'Down Under' for a year, I am glad my little brother doesn't have to deal directly with this international incident. He is a logical, old soul engineer, and this has likely been categorized and placed into his 'too much melodrama' file.

My sister's fiancé has forbidden her to call me anymore; he thinks it is an unnecessary extravagance. Working only intermittently due to a health condition, he mostly lives off her. Onto him the minute we met, I can see his true nature—and he knows it. My sister's loyalty infuriates him; he is jealous of the fact that she is always there for me, no matter the circumstance. His family epitomizes dysfunction and deceit, and he envies our unconditional sibling love and familial integrity.

Unequivocally, I do not want her to marry this man; I have a sickening foreboding of what the future holds for her if she does. He has psychological issues, and is far too controlling. I want to spare her the pain, but just as I did not heed my best friend's warning about my fiancé, my sister will not listen to me. It seems we all need to go through the lessons we are destined to experience. Maybe it is only the supremely wise who circumvent disaster, or choose the judicious fork in the road.

Sketching on my artist's pad at the tiny oceanside thatched-roof bar, I sip an ever-present mineral water with fresh lime. I have discarded my sandals, and wiggle my toes through the cool sand. The waiters find it most odd that I don't indulge in copious amounts of alcohol, as do most foreigners around me. Many modern-day, hippy ex-pats I meet in Old Vallarta drift through their days, weeks, months, and even years without any apparent purpose, imbibing far too much.

Yesterday, I met a girl who had come here to flee heartbreak, and had squandered eight months in the desert-island ambience of Las Ánimas, drinking herself into a stupor. Only in the past week has she returned to Vallarta to dry out, tenuously hanging onto her sobriety. Part of me wishes I could find refuge in a substance, yet, on the other hand, I thank God I do not have an addictive personality. Drugs or alcohol would only exacerbate my emotions and take them to an even more dangerous place. I do not find solace in the unstable sensation of altered states.

Spending the afternoon in solitude, I draw what I see on the beach, and then paint tiny watercolors. My skills are that of a fledgling, but it keeps me occupied and calms my mind. Franco, the waiter, frequently stops by to see what I am doing, and to entertain me with snippets of his life story.

The sun has begun its descent. I gather my things and walk back home along the ocean's edge to soak up a glorious crimson sunset.

My drug of choice is *Dinner and a Movie* marathons, and the Biography Channel. Tonight, I make a simple salad with a quesadilla, and catch a documentary about Paris in the twenties. I am fascinated with this era of writers and artists: Anaïs Nin, Ernest Hemmingway, Henry Miller, F. Scott Fitzgerald, Picasso, Frida Kahlo—and the naughty Josephine Baker. Apparently, Paris was a prodigious sex-fest in the roaring '20s. Parisians eventually tired of the rogues and reprobates and, shortly after WWII began, the debauchery came to a screeching halt when they were all quietly expelled. Paris was never to be the same again, but the epoch altered the landscape of art and literature, capturing our imaginations forever more.

Pepe did not lie; his young sons have not tired of playing dominoes and dice with me when I visit Casa de la Salsa. We have long, lingering games, and they are in no hurry to escape. The waiters greet me as part of the family, giving me preferential treatment, and slipping tasty indulgences onto my table.

Pepe stops in tonight and teaches me a Mexican card game that we play, betting brightly colored candies. Chatting in Spanglish, he talks about his family and his plans for restaurant renovations, and the purchase of a new property. The staff respect and admire him. When it is time to leave, I learn he has covered my bill.

I make my way up the dirty little cobblestone street that I am growing so fond of: passing the hot dog vendor who is lined up with late night feeders, yet stops to smile at me; petting the scruffy little guard dog named Estrella that watches over a tiny tortilla shop; waving to the friendly cook at the corner café who sells tacos made from cow tongue.

"Come to France. I can only assume that, if you don't come, you are with another man," Jean-François says. He has called to campaign once again for my return.

"*Arrêt* Jean-François. I am the one who deserves an explanation, not you."

"Look, there was a huge problem with my divorce. Are you coming back?"

What is wrong with this feckless Frenchman? I have gotten no straight answers, and there is no talk of coming to get me, no offer to send a ticket. Am I supposed to jump on a plane back to the minefield, hoping that I don't get blown up once again? Is he so self-absorbed that he cannot grasp what it was like for me to be banished from France so soon after I arrived? He clearly does not know what a man of honor would do.

My back spasms hard, as it has been doing over the past week, like a vice grip on my spine. The surgery worked wonders up until now; anxiety will always attack the weakest link.

I try to return to my book, but tears spill onto the page. Falling asleep on a soaked pillow, with the sounds of salsa music in the distance, cheery and celebratory for the Day of the Kings, the merriment cannot penetrate my melancholy.

I have hit the bottom of this dense, black bog. Sitting on the edge of a pier off the boardwalk, I watch the pterodactyl-like pelicans dive in their dance for fish.

The foundation of my life has been washed away. In a moment, everything became undone—by my own choices. It was a decent life; I am a stupid girl, as the French shrew so succinctly told me in Paris. I have sold almost everything, and have no home to return to. Precariously, I bob, adrift in the flotsam of this crash.

Why did I shout my love for the Frenchman from the rooftops for the entire world to hear, right down to the dentist and the drycleaner? How can I return? What am I to say after gliding around like a daft idiot in a bubble of giddiness?

I cringe, as Shame enshrouds me, her evil tentacles curling around my body, constricting my breath. Ruthlessly, she squeezes the life force from me, taunting me with insults.

Did you think you deserved your dream of true love?

That it would stick?

That there was going to be a happily ever after?

What a disillusioned fool.

My body convulses as I sob, all of my being steeped in remorse and self-loathing. This epic mistake is unforgivable.

The high priestess of cruelty, Shame's dark mission is destruction.

You are better off dead, she hisses.

Startled, I feel a light touch on my left shoulder. A man, an American, sits down next to me, shattering Shame's spell as she skulks away. He asks if there is anything he can do. That this young man has noticed me at a distance, and has felt compelled to come to my aid, shocks me. I assure him I will be okay, and only after he feels convinced does he leave.

I wipe my face of the spill of tears, spent. Hypnotized by the waves, I hang suspended in a hollow tunnel at hell's door. The water whispers that today I must make a choice. I cannot sustain this level of despair and survive. I must either throw myself into the ocean and end the staggering pain, or find a way to pull myself out of this weighty mire. The desire to stop living pulls at me, the will to exist pushes.

Eventually, a power greater than my grief persuades me to a walk away from the water. Even though I'm not sure how to live, I don't know how to die.

Today is my confession; this is not a call I've looked forward to. Ron has received my letter, but now I must speak to him in person. My stomach churns with nausea as I dial the number.

He wants to hear the story. After I spew, he laughs, and says he and his wife should make a business trip to Mexico to come see me. My stomach stops rolling and my muscles relax. My job is open and they look forward to my return. I can take my original six-month leave of absence as planned, no problem.

Ron wisely suggests that, after such an experience, I may be happier with a change of scenery—a move to Calgary. We will switch things around, and rent a business apartment in Edmonton for the frequent trips I will be making there. It is an excellent idea, and gives me something to look forward to. Calgary is not anything close to the life I had envisioned in Europe, but at least it's a seedling of a new life after my expectations of a sweeping transition.

I should have known he would handle the situation with grace. I am comforted in knowing that one part of my life is safe in the hands of a man I can count on through anything.

Gina, the manicurist at the salon, has invited me to her home for dinner. Just a short walk from the edge of town, she lives in a small apartment along the noisy highway to Mismaloya. We talk about men, and life, and she tells me about her lover, Beto. He appeared at her window last night, drunk, with a band of mariachis in tow to serenade her. This is the Mexican version of buying flowers for bad behavior, except much more dramatic and costly.

Beto is young and an alcoholic. Money is not a problem for him; his family owns a prosperous restaurant, which has guaranteed business from tour groups visiting their jungle town. He works there, and Gina tells me his father spoils him with a large salary for a few hours of work a day.

She and he have had another lover's quarrel, and he is aiming to get back in her good graces. I stare at her, and don't know why she would tolerate one minute of any man's bad behavior, infidelity, or drunkenness. A gaggle of good men would drop at her feet any time, in any country.

The artistic scrawl on a notice posted in Café Amadeus caught my eye a few days ago. Private Spanish classes for $10 an hour at the café. The idea appealed to me; Amadeus is in a grand old whitewashed house located up a steep stairway, sitting in the rock of a hill. It is an oasis of tranquility with its classical-only music and wide open windows.

Beethoven is playing, and the barista has just delivered a cappuccino with a perfect head of dense white foam. My brand new journal, and a turquoise fountain pen sit on the table, one that I sell thousands of back home. On the first page of the book, I write a heading in calligraphy, with swirls and doodles, while I wait. Learning Spanish will help keep my thoughts off negativity; organized activities are good for a wandering mind.

A tall, thin man walks up to my table. He has the appearance of an Indian professor, with a scruffy gray beard and wiry hair. Introducing himself, he shakes my hand with the haughtiness of someone well educated and highly cultured.

Going over my expectations, he then outlines the structure of the classes, and we set up a twice-weekly schedule. Using Madrigal's Spanish, he tests my level of ability, and begins instructing without further adieu.

He is engaging, and I look forward to using more of the language in my day-to-day conversations. His teaching style is firm and productive and, in spite of his snobbishness, I think I will like Rodolfo.

Samuel, the owner of the hotel, has a soft spot for me. He has kindly lent me his CD player; I feel like I've won the lottery. Music is as necessary for my soul as air is for my lungs, and I am relishing the select few albums I brought with me while I paint tonight. I can now listen to French songstresses without breaking down.

A breeze caresses the palm trees on the patio as I mix paint and test new colors. Ever so slightly, my body and spirit mend, stroke by stroke, as I dip my brush onto the palette and paint on the coarse paper. The practice is meditative, and I fashion rudimentary scenes of water, and beaches, and flowers. My mind wanders to the spot on that corner just off the Baixa, where my life intersected with fate, and forever changed.

On numerous occasions, I have requested a reassignment to

a different location when I leave this plane; I love planet Earth and think she is gorgeousness embodied—humanity is another thing. Our entire history is one of barbarism and, no matter how we evolve technologically, we never rise above hatred and idiocy. Humans cannot grasp how everything is connected, and that we are all one.

The possibility that we have to keep returning to this dense (in both senses of the word) planet, to get it right, fills me with consternation. I do not want to be mandated to maneuver through this confusing, pain-filled maze again. Unfortunately, I have found too much evidence to support the theory that we reincarnate, over and over again.

When I met Jean-François, I had a sensation that was utterly unlike any other I had previously experienced in my romantic liaisons, or friendships for that matter. I knew him. He never felt like a stranger to me. It was as though I had found someone who'd been lost; like I'd finally been reunited with a piece of my soul, after a very long time.

To have known someone for so short a period of time, and feel as though your heart has been shattered into shards, makes little sense. Because of its irrationality, it bewilders me deeply. To have found a poignant part of myself, and then to have lost it so suddenly, defies belief.

The French don't say I miss you. They say *tu me manques*, which literally translates to 'you are missing from me.' My vacant energy is such, because he is missing from me, like a limb, like precious sight.

Open Air Expeditions is close to Café Amadeus, and today I stop in. Focusing on helping something or someone, rather than regurgitating my own sad story, would be a step in the right direction. I hope to volunteer; I will swab the decks, or do anything to assist in their efforts with the whales and dolphins. I don't swim well and am afraid of deep water, but I adore going out on *top* of the waves to find sea life. The whales come down from Canada to have their babies here, and they have always been dear to my heart. It would be wonderful to be involved in any efforts to keep them safe in the Bay of Banderas.

A marine biologist is in, and spends two hours discussing the whales in the bay; seventy-three have been identified, and he explains their various fluke markings in the photos covering the walls. He is kind to take the time with me. I want to do something productive while I am here, but unfortunately there is no opportunity for me to help out.

I meander the hills until dusk and, after watching the sun set into the ocean, eat at the counter of a corner taco stand with Mexican workmen, indulging in jumbo shrimp tacos and a cold *cerveza*. I am thankful for the fresh food, for the sound of the men bantering in Spanish, for being directed to come to a place that feels like home in my heart.

Gabriel, the handyman, is at my door, and I tell him that my phone is married. With a straight face, he politely shakes his head, telling me he doesn't understand. The phone is not functioning, and the Spanish dictionary reveals my ridiculous error.

Reluctantly, I moved from the large 'penthouse' to a tiny room next door, but the hotel has kindly repainted it for me, put in a new phone, a television, and two ceiling fans. Rent for the smaller space is brilliantly low, and they have also agreed to do my laundry in-house. The staff are cordial, and forgiving of my

Spanish. I feel like *la princesa* of the Paloma—a broken princess in a humble abode, but a princess nonetheless.

No longer able to cook for myself in the kitchen-less room, I've deemed this evening a treat night. Vallarta has become more sophisticated since my last visit three years ago. A new breed of elegant restaurants with international cuisine has cropped up, and it's hard to keep my nose out of them.

Café des Artistes has a lush, flower-filled garden in the back and, in the evenings, a pianist plays soft, soul-soothing music, so I sit at the bar with a glass of buttery chardonnay, and read a letter that has arrived from Monique in the mail.

> *Dear Wanda,*
>
> *Paris is already warming. The past week has been gorgeous, and today is exceptionally beautiful with a gentle rain. We have the most romantic sunsets, and I am discovering new sights with Denise.*
>
> *How are you doing? Any word from Jean-François? Is my mail reaching you? What are your thoughts at the moment? Are you slowly finding a path through your quagmire? Perhaps you have met a nice man to divert your thoughts for a while ...*

Interrupted by the arrival of a decadent meal with filet mignon and wild mushrooms in burgundy sauce, I briefly stop, and then pick up the pages once more.

Monique further writes of a recent, racy rendezvous with her lover, Florentin. Her life in Paris is so completely divergent to anyone's back home, and her letters are delicious novelettes. The dramas at the hammam, a Turkish bathhouse where people liaise and lustfully interact, read like a soap opera. Always something fascinating afoot, French life suits my dear friend well.

Peeling the dry sheaths off the green *tomatillos*, I dice them at a cooking class with an open bar, mildly inebriated. Women surround me sipping massive margaritas, and the restaurateur, who is holding the class, is basking in the limelight.

Our instructions are on various fresh and roasted salsas, all flavorful. The menu includes chicken enchiladas in mole sauce, with even more margaritas. The dish is scrumptious, but we have not been given a recipe, or directions on how to make the mole, so everyone is let down.

After class, four stragglers—all single women—carry on at a nearby blues bar. Guillermo, our instructor, joins us. When the others are not looking, he slips a card into the palm of my hand.

> *Would you like me to give you the mole*
> *recipe over dinner one night?*
> *Call me.*
> *Guillermo.*

The mole was good, but certainly not worth an evening of pomposity. He is not appealing, in spite of how he feels about his own charm and local 'fame.'

One of the women is too drunk to walk, and Guillermo feels responsible, but is none too pleased that he has to leave and escort her home in a taxi.

Passing by La Dolce Vita on the long stroll home, I stop in at the urging of a waiter with an offer of a late night sambuca. A group of swarthy Italians invite me to join them, and a longhaired, pretty Italian hair stylist, who has recently moved to Vallarta, starts a private conversation with me. Three Mexican men join the table, and one orders me another sambuca.

The night has slipped into *la madrugada*, so I say my farewells, and the Mexican who ordered the second drink escorts me back to the hotel in a most gentlemanly manner, ensuring I arrive safely.

Rodolfo and I settle in with our cappuccinos to begin my Spanish class at Café Amadeus. He mentioned my query to his wife; after the last class I asked if he had any offers, and suggested a buy-ten-get-one-free idea; a very Canadian thing to propose. He balked at the idea. His wife, however, thinks it is clever, and that he should offer it to all of his students. He says that she would like to meet me.

Rodolfo intently observes me under his sleepy-eyed gaze while I recite my Spanish homework. He is assessing me. I have said nothing of France, and today after our lesson and a brief history of Mexico, he tells me the tale of him and his wife.

Her name is Vivienne and she is French. While traveling on a train through the northern countryside of Italy, they met and became lovers. They too continued a long distance love affair, and she visited Mexico on a two-week vacation. After returning to France, she knew she had fallen in love with Rodolfo, and that she longed for a change in lifestyle. Through many discussions and phone calls declaring their love for each other, she sold her Paris apartment, gave up a successful career in music, and her life in France, to come to Mexico.

He confides that, secretly, he was terrified to marry again, and did not want to change his life. The responsibility of a woman coming from a foreign country and giving up her life solely for him felt frightening. The day before the flight, he called her to ask if she was still really coming, but in fact, he didn't want her to. At the final moment, he decided it would be too cruel, too shocking for Vivienne, after all of their extensive planning, their longing, and their love, to say so.

"Sometimes, a man has to have *huevos*."

She arrived with twelve large boxes; he panicked when he saw them at her side. But he never said anything to her. In due time, he calmed himself, and everything worked out. Now they have a small family with a six-month-old baby named Tula, and a green-eyed cat called Chou Chou.

Eyes wide, I sit flabbergasted by the unbelievable irony. The difference is that Jean-François did not have any qualms about the shit storm he set into motion, and had absolutely no impulse to grab his *huevos*.

Weeks ago, I stopped in at Galería Uno with some of my small watercolors; now that I am slightly saner, I am mortified that I, somehow, thought they might deem the work worthy of placing in a gallery.

Mon Dieu.

It is astonishing how one's perception can become exceedingly skewed under duress. Kudos for the owner's graciousness—I don't know what I would have done if I were an art expert and someone walked in with such absurdly amateurish work. She was more than kind to me. Maybe she, too, sensed my fragility and did not want to make things worse.

It was on good instinct that I came to this country. Slowly and steadily, the sun, in its infinite capacity, helps to heal wounds that seem un-healable. The soul of the land holds ancient remedies for body and spirit. The people, so different from my own, will not allow forlorn anonymity. They cannot walk past anguish or ignore despair. They coax life out of the injured with compassion.

I have cried enough.

Venturing away from the city for day trips, last week I traveled north to Rincon de Guayabitos, where I picked tiny shells along the shoreline and played fetch with a golden retriever. The week before, I went to watch the high waves of Sayulita. Both areas attract surfers and have grand expanses of beach to walk.

Yesterday, I whale watched under the shoreline *palapas* at Punta de Mita with Karin, a new acquaintance, and a group of her German friends.

Today, I am in San Pancho, a sleepy little village, with only a few rustic cafés and a dilapidated convenience store.

A huge cockatoo struts freely about the restaurant and flies high up into a palm tree. After a late lunch of shrimp ceviche, I visit the pet monkey that is tied to a leash in front of the restaurant. I *hate* seeing wild animals chained, but at least she has a nice ocean view.

As we play, she eyes my curls, and then deftly leaps onto the top of my head. Planting herself, she grabs reams of long hair in both hands and both feet, and pulls in either direction. Hard. Gently, I try to unclench her hands to no avail, looking over at the owner for help. He shrugs with an expression that says, *you're the stupid tourist who got yourself into this mess; you get yourself out of it.* He walks back into the kitchen, unfazed.

The monkey is thoroughly enjoying this game. I, on the other hand, realize that I am at the mercy of a wild animal that may be, understandably, harboring a grudge against my kind. A mild panic sets in, and then I determine it best to say 'uncle.' Surrendering, I sit down on the cement fence to wait it out. Eventually, she tires of the ruse and climbs down off my head, obviously pleased with herself.

Lesson learned.

Sitting under massive palm fronds on a patio, Dauro, the gorgeous longhaired Italian hairstylist, and Giuseppe, an older, crinkly-brown Italian on vacation from Sicily, entertain me. Dauro has been flirting with me; he sweetly stirs the doldrums where my deflated ego drifts. Passing by his salon on the way from the beach, I stopped in and was invited to dinner.

Giuseppe is freshly shaven, and appears to have gotten a haircut after I left for the hotel to shower and change for the evening. At an outdoor Brazilian barbeque, the waiters appear every few minutes with swords of aromatic grilled meats, while Giuseppe does his best to charm me. Bit by bit, Dauro backs off, much to my dismay.

Moving to La Dolce Vita for drinks, the moment we are alone, Dauro asks if I am interested in Giuseppe. Trying not to look horrified, I tell him, absolutely not. Instantly, he warms with the confirmation that he is not stepping on his friend's toes. My insides fill with butterflies when, each time I mention a friend in the conversation, he says in his melodious Italian accent, "Is she as beautiful as you?" I find it hard to believe this Adonis finds me beautiful.

My skin carries the ache of relentless yearning from what was ripped away like a bandage, and I am stung with a jolt of electricity each time he touches my arm. I realize I am in a position of vulnerability, and that I have a precarious neediness right now.

Looking into his eyes, I know my heart could easily attach itself to this man, with one likely outcome. All of my life it has been this way: a swelling, a falling, and then a disappointing shatter. Further battered and cracked with each loss, my heart feels as though the pieces that fall off will never, ever grow back. How much can the human heart withstand? I want to know how to survive, not unscathed (no one is), but far less damaged. I seem not to know how to safeguard my crystalline heart.

A secret stash of sundried olives and aged cheeses arrive at the table with baskets of hot bread and small bowls of balsamic and oil. Dauro's friends join us, and the tempo of the conversation rises, mesmerizing me with the singsong sound of the language, which is continually punctuated by wild gesticulations. I have determined that Italian men are my favorite in the world. They so fully embody their masculinity, and are not afraid to show their appreciation of a woman.

The last of the diners have left, and the owners of La Dolce join us for drinks. They have hit the sweet spot of success with this brilliant idea of authentic Italian fare in Mexico, wisely hiring amiable waiters who are experts at their trade.

Insistent on my safety, the entire Italian contingent drops me off at the hotel lobby in the middle of an extraordinary Mexican night.

February / Febrero

The wound is the place where the light enters you.
—Rumi

THE MIND IS A TANGLED AND SECRETIVE PLACE. RELUCTANTLY, it reveals our deepest complexities, and it is only because of long periods of silence that mine has begun to speak. Aside of love-craziness, my motivations are becoming clearer to me.

Every fall the cold comes and, quickly following it, the snow. Layering myself in heavy clothing; chipping ice from my car; driving through an arctic cement jungle from place to place; maneuvering around three foot snow drifts on hazardous highways—the people around me don't seem to find it absurd. In spite of the certainty of winter, I am forever caught off guard, unprepared to face the harshness of it all over again. Lost for many long months in hibernation, I labor to create an artificial sense of happiness, year after year, in this shades-of-blue season.

At Safeway, I buy plastic fruit and packaged meat from mills, and the only way I get fresh, locally grown produce is at summer markets with sky-high prices. I eat at restaurants with mediocre food staged as something grandiose, and waitresses who expect large tips for short skirts and deep cleavage, but they never remember that I have been there before.

In the extended period of darkness and cold, I get my exercise in a sterile gym, surrounded by serious and stern people who grunt and groan, but don't speak.

It has become clear to me now, that I work hard and smart for one reason only, aside of basic necessities—for the freedom to see and experience the world. Not homes, not cars, not an amassment of the material; my first and foremost value in life is flying away to places that match my frequency. Many people love winter, many people enjoy their corporate jobs, and many people prefer the structure of our society. Those who do are living their truth, and that is as it should be, but my soul knows that I am, at a deep level, an imposter; that I am perpetrating a ruse. Reflecting, I realize that meaningless work, for me, is a waste of precious life.

Here, I have time to talk to a diversity of fascinating characters, strangers who all have their own unique life story to tell me. Here, I walk consciously, observing intricate details I dash past in that other life. A natural night owl, here, I don't need to conform to the dogma, which intimates that I am lazy for a having a different inner-biorhythmic clock than the norm. Here, I eat real food that is harvested nearby; food that nourishes the body, and tastes the way nature intended. Sidestepping the road most traveled for a small stretch right now, I learn new things and unfamiliar ways of being, in the style of slow Latin life, a place where time is fluid.

On this little blue planet, we are born and set adrift, without a map, instructions, or paddles—without any relevant information about why we are here. The harsh face-off with my mortality so early carried a small set of directions, and valuable clues about my existence. This fiasco reminds me, once again, that time on Earth is fleeting, and that we have a bounty of magic we are free to experience before we leave.

Fantasies of flitting off that were first awakened in Greece,

I now realize, have long simmered in the seat of my soul. Not only did Jean-François fill a dearth of sensuous pleasure and unabashed joy, he gave me an excuse—a valid reason to do something unconventional and uncommon—to live my truth instead of my indoctrination.

In a few months, I must return to the life that I wanted to leave—a lifestyle that I intuitively understand has contributed to my maladies. My mind was set on the opportunity for a healthier, happier way of being, and it was stolen before it could begin. Not only has love evaporated, the adventure into my *real* life will soon be over. Disappointment exacerbates my still lingering lovesickness.

I must write a new story, although where to begin I am unsure.

Another letter has arrived from my little brother. On the extreme budget plan, he eats boxes of macaroni and cheese, and vegemite sandwiches (even the ones he found ants in), far away in The Land Down Under. Working on a commune-style farm, it's vaguely worrisome, because of the over-the-top religious tone of the place. My calamity is enough; I hope we don't have to rescue him there. Away on a year of profound soul searching, he needs to assert his independence. While he's been finding himself, I've lost myself. But I am gently recovering her.

Following his letter was another from my sister. She says our mum is on a road trip to Belize with her partner. I am pleased to hear this; she is on a new journey, with a new man. Had she not gotten a divorce, she would not be taking any foreign vacations, and she has always dreamed of traveling.

Because I am so far away, and her friends are all preoccupied or missing in action, my sister, Lana, is pouting. She wants help with the details of her wedding plans. Even though I am her maid of honor, I dread this forthcoming marriage.

This little hotel is a bizarre blend of pamper and privation. Even though I have pleaded for hot water, I shower under a cold, weak spray most days. Getting a fresh towel is a challenge. Yet, I can take a huge sack of dirty clothing to the *lavandería* and have them done the same day, and returned to me in a neatly folded pile with the scent of fresh laundry—all for less than three dollars.

But Adriana, the manager, works hard and, for a young woman, helms the ship well. I watch Samuel, the owner, watch her, and I see a tenderness in his eyes. Married, she is out of bounds, but I am certain he is in love with her.

Downstairs in the lobby, I search every corner for my little black address book. I learn that the night clerk tossed it in the garbage last night, and now all of my precious contact information is gone. An English-speaking woman at the front desk is playing a game of charades in an attempt to get towels from Olivia, to no avail. With an imminent brunch reservation, she needs to take a shower. In Spanish, I let our 'clerk-concierge' know of her predicament. She says in five minutes they will have towels.

"In five Mexican minutes, you'll get your towels," I say.

Olivia, the front desk clerk who has not spoken a word of English to me, mysteriously understands this comment and laughs, wagging a finger at me.

Annette introduces herself, thanks me, and invites me to a mariachi brunch with her and a friend. At first declining, I quickly change my mind, realizing it would be good to have a festive breakfast with women.

The two, it turns out, are from the city where I will be transferring to upon my return home. Bubbly, full-figured brunettes—both lifeguards, much to my surprise—they are enjoying Vallarta's climate and charm.

Sunday breakfast in this popular tourist place is an event, with a ten-piece mariachi band, and a massive buffet. The girls have rented a jeep and invite me on a day trip out of town with a couple they know, she from Canada and he, a local. After a slow stroll, I join them for an afternoon at the beach, and I am amused by Rita's colorful Carmen Miranda sunhat covered in flowers. It seems at least twenty-five years ahead of her age. To each her own.

An oddly matched couple arrives at the hotel to fetch us in an open-air jeep. He is a young, virile looking Mexican with a severe military-style haircut and sharp, indigenous features. She, Lynn, is a self-assured, striking blonde, who eyes me suspiciously, and appears irritated by having to participate in this adventure. I sense that she has either been coerced, or is doing it out of obligation.

Hair blowing wildly, we drive out to the towns north of the city, and stop for a beer at a sleepy beach in Punta de Mita. Fishermen are fussing with their small *panga* boats and nets, and only a few tourists sit under the *palapas*.

The girls know Lynn through a personal development course she facilitates. I learn that she and Pablo spend six months in Mexico while he works, and then six months in Canada where she works. A rather brilliant arrangement; she gets a six-month holiday away from the hell of winter, as does he in a Canadian summer, plus neither needs to go through the hassle of a work visa.

Lynn and Pablo live a skip up the hill from Paloma del Mar and, in spite of her frosty demeanor, I like her. Suggesting that we meet one day for lunch—I need more women here—I am pleased she agrees to it.

A colony of artists paint daily in the tranquil courtyard of the Pueblo Reale. Edgar, a quiet, talented fellow teaches in oil, and I have begun classes with him. The instruction is strictly in Spanish. Across from his studio is a small, quaint café with aromatic Chiapas coffee, home-baked pastries, and an always-fresh fruit plate, so this is where I take my breakfasts before class begins.

One of the artists, Caesar, paints tiny watercolors, and sells many of them to the tourists. He seems most discontented and works with a scowl; in actuality, he is a pleasant and friendly sort once you get to know him.

Keeping myself amused, I paint little scenes for friends and family, and mail them off. I have switched mediums; I find watercolor too bland and washed out for my tastes or, I suppose, for my level of understanding and ability. I am painting a pretty Mexican terra cotta doorway, and I love the vibrantly rich colors, and the feel of the thick paint. The layering and the slow strokes are soothing, and Edgar's silent energy is calming and strong. I feel like a child, but that's to be expected when we first try anything. *Poco a poco*, I shall learn. It's slow progress, but it doesn't matter. I have no mission—my main purpose is therapy.

✛ *Au nom du Père, et du Fils, et du Saint-Esprit. Amen.* ✛ Passing the church of Guadalupe on the bus, I mindlessly follow the Mexicans' lead, with the sign of the cross. Reminiscing of Portugal today, the recitations of the French priests in St. Boniface, where my grandfather lived, spring to mind.

God and I are on speaking terms again. I do not understand the path of my life, however I cannot live without faith, and the belief that there is a reason for everything, with a divine force that assists me in times of need—one that responds to my gratitude, and to my prayers. I don't believe in the God of my childhood: a man in the sky with human emotions, a jealous and angry God, who is somehow pleased when we quake in fear of him. I don't buy warped, manmade interpretations of the bible, the ones constructed to manipulate and control. I do believe there is much, much more than what we see. Jesus told us we could do all he did and greater— he, the man who walked on water, and manifested fishes and loaves.

As sad as I have been, as betrayed as I have felt, I take accountability for my decision. When I opted to go to France, I knew I was taking a fifty-fifty chance. God had nothing to do with my freewill, and did not interfere with the choices I made.

In hindsight, I realize I did not properly communicate with Jean-François. An oversight on my part, I did not tell him that I was arriving with enough funds to cover my six-month visit. I knew he was stressed about his divorce proceedings just prior to my arrival, but in my excitement, I did not want to sully the romance of the moment with financial matters. Conveying this may have quelled any concerns he had, but didn't express. It doesn't excuse his bad behavior, but I wish I'd have been clear about my ability to take care of my own needs.

Even though I understand this, it is not a salve for the tears and fissures on my heart. I do not know if time shall heal these wounds, but I pray that it will.

Awakening every morning to a pure blue sky and a smiling sun, I cannot blame any of my moods on the weather.

Earth tremors have been rumbling and, a few nights ago, one woke me. Today, a mild earthquake was reported, but sitting on the beach, I didn't feel it. Kevin, a fellow Canadian, was injured in a quake here two years ago, and says, when he arrived at the hospital, a representative from the Canadian Consulate was already there with a copy of his insurance, and had everything under control, so he was quickly attended to. He had no idea how she knew, but she brought flowers, came twice a day to visit, and arranged for a flight home to Canada when he was fully recovered.

After a short visit with Kevin on my way to Playa de los Muertos, I spot Susan at the beach bar in front of her hotel. She has arrived for a family vacation, and has brought me a book called *Simple Abundance*. She says it may help with my healing. Giving me a handful of pens to give away here, she tells me the latest news of work: gossip, changes, and trade shows that I will be working when I return to my territory. I, in turn, tell her all that I've done since my unexpected sojourn in Mexico. It is wonderful to see her, to chitter chatter with a good friend once again.

Letters from friends continue to come via fax and post. A newsy missive arrives from Teresa today. She finally received the letter, poem, and painting I sent, and said she only got as far as the bench in front of the post office to read it. Shari has been writing lovely and encouraging letters on cheery stationery, Arlene sends funny cards, and Lynnette calls.

After a discussion with her French friend, Julia, Lana sent a long letter about the cultural differences between Canada and France. She told Julia of Jean-François' comments during our brief interlude in France together. Julia prefaced her overview of the French with the fact that she is generalizing, but shed light on the cultural nuances.

French women are mostly thin, and take pride in looking impeccable at all times; appearance is of utmost importance, and the men feed into the notion of their women looking immaculate.

Point of interest: an anklet is a sign of a prostitute in France.

Julia said it would be extremely hard for someone as head-strong as I am to be authentically myself there, because Jean-François would feel obligated to teach me the ways of being a proper French woman, and that it would be embarrassing for him if I were to behave and dress too much as my Canadian self. I would most likely be pressured to keep the home, my appearance, and my behavior as the French do. She feels my creativity and my deep values around friendships would be squashed. She also speculated that men over forty are typically jealous and possessive. When being instructed on how to dress and act 'appropriately,' I would need to relinquish any tendencies to take it personally.

How naïve we can be. Aside of what I read of in *Culture Shock! France*, I never considered the nuances of cultural mores and unspoken rules—and that Jean-François would expect me to adhere to them. If I were to move to France alone, I could choose to act and dress whichever way I pleased, as Monique does. But under the thumb of a Frenchman, it seems I would need to acquiesce to his ways if I wanted harmony.

I cannot imagine it—submissiveness has never been one of my character traits. My mother does not get away with telling me what to do; a man would never be able to reign me into adhering to a rigid set of ridiculous rules. I do not believe I came to Earth in this particular lifetime to live under domination, stifled and suffocated. There is far too much gypsy in my soul for that.

Each day at the Burro Bar, 'Zsa Zsa Gabor' makes an entrance in gold lame getups or animal print bikinis, laden with faux jewels, her skin tanned to a coffee-brown leather hide. She is a spirited and wild character who loves Mexican cocktails. An aging German blonde bombshell with a younger, doting husband, Karin is fun to be with in short spells, but gets aggressive, waving her fists when making a point after too many margaritas.

Saturday, I got caught in a tropical rainstorm with flash flooding that swelled into rivers running through the cobblestone streets. Storm-stayed in Gringo Gulch, where Americans swarm and loiter, I ran into Karin and a motley crew of characters. The rain was spectacular, and it was with great amusement that I watched the prissiest of women being forced to abandon their shoes and roll up their pants, trudging barefoot through the gushing water.

Today, I join Karin's friends for poolside drinks at their hotel. At the precise moment I walk up the stairs of the hotel, unbeknownst to me, a man is getting out of a taxi across the street. He has just arrived from the airport for a vacation with his new wife, and she is unaware of his motive for choosing Puerto Vallarta. He spots me—the object of his decision to come here—on the stairs. Of all the hotels, all the cafes, bars, and restaurants, all of the beaches, and streets I could be on at this *momentito*, I am entering this hotel at the exact time he has arrived at his.

At the pool, I am greeted by a welcoming, animated group of German women. I learn that one sparkly blonde with pale blue eyes is married to a much younger Mexican man. She moved here from Canada to teach, and fell in love along the way.

As I regale the group with a story, a strong presence behind me gives pause to my banter, and a shadow falls. I turn, leaping off my chair—and almost out of my skin.

It is none other than my ex-husband, Terry.

He asks if we can talk away from the group. Here with his wife for a vacation, he came specifically to check up on me. My sister revealed to him what had happened, and he knows my grand adventure has gone terribly sideways. He also knows me well, and understands how profoundly my heart wounds. Another epic break up so soon after us, he realizes, could be dangerous to my state of mind. He has come to ensure, firsthand, that I am okay.

In a way that I didn't think possible, I forgave his transgressions, and we have remained friends. I am stunned to see him, and moved that he would come all the way to Mexico to check on me. He says he will call me at the hotel later in the week to chat again.

Sitting under a cool banyan tree by the river at Cuizas, I read *Toujours Provence*, a treasure that was hiding with the dictionaries at Una Página en el Sol (A Page in the Sun).

Kevin stops by to debrief; he and I went on a dinner date last week, and then back to his loft apartment for a deep discussion about relationships. Well over budget, we got into wine, margaritas, and then dinner aperitifs. Two of his friends dropped by, and they all coaxed me to go to the local gay club for stripper night. All had a crazy time, and I left them still dancing—shirtless-ly—at 4:30 a.m.

Adan, my waiter, spends the rest of my lunch trying to convince me to give him another chance. He had asked me out on a date two weeks ago, and sings a bullshit story over why he stood me up. It is hard to say no when I look into his stunning emerald eyes and chiseled, café-mocha face, but I have no further interest in flaky men.

Old dogs roam the dusty streets, and Wild West cantina doors conceal the activities of the men-only bars inside. I have been transported back in time into old-world Mexico.

I accepted the invitation to come to Santa Maria del Oro to stay for a long weekend with my new German friend, Katarina, and her sullen young Mexican husband. The name she goes by is Petruwich. Her parents had planned to name her Katarina, but because Hitler did not like Katarina the Great, people were not permitted to name their babies such (was there no end to that tyrant's insanity?). She uses Katarina when singing, or signing her art, so I shall call her by the glorious name she was originally to have been christened with.

Their small casa is adobe, and deceptively ordinary on the outside. Inside, is an artistic, European world of color and design. The backyard is a wild jungle-garden, with a large orange tree, tangled bushes, gargantuan flowers, and a beckoning hammock.

I am fascinated by the age gap and contrasts between this couple, who somehow connected, fell in love, and married. She is a sturdy-looking blonde German of fifty-four, and he is a standard model Mexican of twenty-nine. Continually bubbling, she is full of ideas, creativity, and life. Brooding and moody for no ostensible reason, he is the type of man I want to kick in the pants. How can anyone so young take himself so seriously?

With the huge generational gap, the frame of reference between a man and woman from the same country could be a challenge in and of itself, but add to that the cultural differences, and my curiosity is piqued around the communication between the two, and what they may have in common.

I change into a short denim dress to go for a walk in the blistering heat, and Katarina raises her brows, asking if I am certain that this is what I plan to wear. Apparently, such a dress will cause a stir in this staunchly Catholic, highly conservative town. My body runs hot, and I don't have anything less leg-revealing to wear, so we must face the disapproval of the town's people—not that I care a fig.

Passing a cluster of nuns, we meander down the hill to the center of town. I cannot imagine what I would do in this tiny backwater town, so far away from modern society.

My feet and ankles are covered in powdery dust when we return home from the walkabout. Katarina quickly cooks a dinner of delicate quesadillas that make only a marginal dent in my hunger. She and her husband are obviously light eaters, so I must go to get groceries in the morning. I don't want to eat them out of house and home, nor do I want to be in a perpetual state of hypoglycemia.

Katarina shows me the compelling art and clever crafts she has made through her treasure hunting; she is a resourceful and imaginative woman. Tomorrow, we will go for a Sunday jaunt to the nearby lake where women must be fully clothed to swim. I cannot fathom being under surveillance, having everything I do assessed, and undoubtedly gossiped about. I would inevitably become the scandal of the town before long. Luckily, I'll be heading out of Dodge before that happens.

The magnitude of his decision has finally hit Jean-François. On the phone, justifying his choices, he says that with the circumstances of living in a cramped apartment, the divorce problems, and his trip to India, he did not want to be the cause of my unhappiness. I tell him that I would have managed, and I cannot stop myself from saying that "*à cause de toi,*" I have been wounded beyond anything else in my life.

Aside of finances, I also see the grand mistake I made in not telling him my thoughts and plans for freelance writing, in detail. Evidently, he does not know me well enough to grasp how independent I am, likely suspicious that I was coming with the notion of being a kept woman.

Hanging up, my heart is assuaged a fragment. He very much wants me back, but I will not take that risk. I will *not* be tossed aside twice.

Not feeling as well as usual—I have had many headaches, my hair has been falling out since I got here, and a thick grey streak suddenly appeared on the crown of my head, seemingly overnight. I pray that I survive this without triggering another cancer.

March / Marzo

The sun shall always rise upon a new day and there shall always be a rose garden within me. Yes, there is a part of me that is broken, but my broken soil gives way to my wild roses.
—C. JoyBell C.

HER FACE IS A MAP OF STORIES, AND SHE SAGS WITH THE excess weight on her body, as she cooks at this tiny taco stand. She loves to gossip; I understand bits of her tales, as she calls various men bastards and assholes. Her plump daughter feigns interest, while she takes a fourth sample of the thick *birria* stew. Has any man ever made love to this old woman? Truly loved and adored her? Or has she only mated with machos, men who have left her wanting and empty? There is no trace of her youth beneath the lines and furrows, so I don't know if she was a beauty. No matter, every woman alive deserves to be deeply loved, to have a man adore her, just for her being-ness.

I leave the taco stand and, on the other side of the street, my ex-husband walks hand in hand with his wife. He waves without her noticing. It would be best if she never recognizes me. I am a thorn in her side and I cannot blame her; in his own way, he still loves me, and she can sense it. She need not worry, but she has no way of knowing that I will never revisit our relationship.

When he and I announced our engagement, and I asked one of my best friends to stand up as a bridesmaid, she refused. Seven years earlier, we had made a pact that I had conveniently forgotten: if either of us were to get engaged to a man we believed was not the right man, or a good man, we would tell the other. So adamant were we that we wrote out promissory notes, signed and dated them, and tucked them into our lingerie drawers.

She told me she could not condone my marriage. Reminding me of our agreement, and her obligation, she warned me that I should not marry this man. He had proven himself to have a philandering inclination once before, and I'd broken up with him because of it. For a year, he persistently pursued me, following his indiscretion and, eventually, I succumbed to his declarations of love—and his boyish charm.

Incensed by her pronouncement, I idealistically assumed that, with the proposal, he had every intention of being faithful. He loved me and I loved him and that was all that mattered. If only we could hear sage advice when it is given. Much to my regret, Tracy and I never spoke again.

Every morning at 7:30 sharp, Tammy Wynette would whine *Stand by Your Man* from the old AM radio in my father's bathroom while he shaved, and I would swoon—in whatever way a seven year old can—dreaming of that boy I could sing about. Maybe lasting, epic love, without a myriad of conditions, is as rare as Hailey's Comet. Why do some have the privilege of love 'til death do they part, while others flounder in an arid wasteland?

This is the greatest mystery of my life.

Lynn and I have been meeting for lunches, and evening walks down the *malecón*. Sleeping in late every day, she goes to the rooftop of their apartment to sun bake all afternoon, and is as brown as a berry. She is a woman who lives life to her own authentic beat, without excuse or apology.

In conversation, I learn that what I thought was disapproval, was actually her private (and flattering) musing on our jeep journey: *Who in the hell invited Marilyn Monroe? I thought she was dead.*

Ironically, we live a block away from each other here in Vallarta, and in Calgary we will be residing in the same neighborhood, within walking distance from one another. The many parallels are striking: we are both the eldest of three, with a sister close in age, and a brother a generation apart; we were married on the same day in September; our fathers are both French, and were born a short distance from each other; our mothers are of British descent; and we were both conceived in a car on a country road in Saskatchewan, less than a couple of years apart.

Today, we have come to Mismaloya to the restaurant where Gina's wayward boyfriend works. Famous for their colossal prawns, we agree they are divine. Cockatoos roam the terra cotta floors, and a tropical garden is in full bloom on a massive patio behind the restaurant.

Taking our time to investigate the area, we meander down dusty roads, perusing street side *tiendas*, and then walk back to the highway to catch the bus. Her clingy boyfriend is not crazy about the time we spend together, but I'm sure she is unconcerned about his petty annoyances.

The femininity of Mexico nourishes broken places within: the lapping of the ocean; the scents and sounds of the jungle; the surrounding Sierra Madres; the wildlife that I am unconnected to in my city life. I will return too soon to a masculine and harsh place, with its concrete walls and money mantra.

It has been an enchanting way to spend a day on planet Earth.

A girl from Alaska is alone and petitions help to navigate Vallarta after an art workshop at Terra Noble, a place nestled high in the hillside with a breathtaking vista overlooking the Bay of Banderas. I volunteer, taking her on a walking tour, and then onto a series of gallery openings, where ex-pats pretend to be art literate while guzzling free, boxed wine served in plastic glasses.

Marta Gilbert, a popular local artist, has already sold most of her new works, and the exhibit has only been open for an hour. Ever the sales person, I calculate a $35,000 night for Marta, thus far. She has long dark hair, looks somewhat Liz Taylor-esque, and appears to be high. I contemplate what it would be like to experience such heady success at art, but I do not believe I would succumb to the temptations and allure of the mind-altering substances that one finds with fame.

Rodolfo and Vivienne's apartment is located near *el centro*, up a winding hill on an über quaint walking-only street. Invited to dinner, I am excited to eat a home cooked meal again.

The two-story apartment is charming—an inviting French-Mexican oasis, a medley of color and culture. Off to the left in the living room, chalky blue stairs with plants and candles littering each step lead to the bedrooms. Both are artists, as is one of Rodolfo's daughters, who studies art in Spain. The place is a veritable gallery. I want to live in this apartment. I could move in and be content exactly as it is.

Vivienne is skinny, has long, wiry, blondish hair, and a huge smile. Her Parisian accent is a reminder of Jean-François, and is oddly comforting. She cooks and sings in the kitchen, while I take my Spanish class with Rodolfo over the tea and cake she has placed next to us.

She is warm and welcoming, and her cooking is delicious and wholesome. Tonight, she has made a luscious guava pie for dessert. We drink wine, and they share many stories of their personal histories, their cultures, their most intimate indiscretions.

Vivienne proudly shows me photos of her home-birth. Their baby, Tula, is Rodolfo's thirteenth child. While married to his previous wife, he also had a *segunda*—an unofficial second 'wife' (a common situation in Mexico)—who bore him children as well. Even though he is sixty-four and Vivienne is almost thirty years younger, I can understand why she fell in love with him. I must admit I have a platonic crush on him, and I think it may be mutual; he has been vying for my attention like a boy, and was petulant when I did not notice one of his many paintings. I already love them both.

They tell me that they were drawn to each other by their love of classical music. Rodolfo was a successful concert cellist a number of years ago, before retiring, and Vivienne was an accomplished conductor before she left France.

This is no easy life for her. She appears undernourished, and must carry laundry and groceries up and down the steep hills, in addition to making all of their food from scratch. She doesn't complain, even though she lived a life of privilege in Europe.

The risk she took to be with him, coming to Mexico from France to be with a man who had sired twelve children with two women simultaneously, was massive. I am placated to learn that I am not the only woman I know to take a ludicrous leap of faith for love.

They open another bottle of wine, and we listen to nasty French songs, which Rodolfo explains imply carnal taboos, yet are popular in France.

Although a lone traveler, one thing I crave is a sense of community in my life. Vivienne and Rodolfo give me that here and now.

As the temperature climbs, my hemlines rise. On the hilly back-streets, I one day stumbled upon a tiny shop with a seamstress who will sew any design of dress you can dream up. The fabric here is inexpensive, as are her services. I bring photos from magazines, and draw pictures, and Rosa creates with surprising accuracy. It is a delightful indulgence to have custom dresses made for so little. There's just one catch: one must return three and four times before the work is completed. I ask for the exact day I should return—I tell her any day is acceptable—and, each time, she smiles and assures me my order will be ready on the day she quotes, and each time it is not.

I discuss this with a new Mexican friend, trying to understand this cultural glitch. It is common to get a yes to many questions, when, in actuality, the answer is no. Or, like the seamstress, the time or the day is far off the mark.

My friend has a most interesting theory: he thinks that, because of the Spanish Inquisition, the Mexican people became conditioned to reply to all questions with the answer the Spaniards wanted to hear, no matter what. He thinks it is something that has been genetically embedded and, when foreigners ask questions, the automatic response is to tell them whatever they want to hear. Who knows if it's true, but it does, hypothetically, hold merit.

A fax has arrived from my sister.

Guess what? I'm coming to Mexico, whether you like it or not. I shouldn't really spend anything extra right now, but I want one last trip with my glorious sister before I get married. Not that we can't go again; it's just that you'll have to carry one of the kids in your backpack by then.

Question Hour:

1) What did you decide about your bridesmaid dress?

2) Do you need anything from Canada?

3) Can I live on fifty cents a day?

4) How much are margaritas?

5) Do I have to sleep with the geckos?

April / Abril

You can cut all the flowers, but you cannot keep spring from coming.
—Pablo Neruda

DAURO HAS BEDDED ME. IT WAS SWEET, BUT UNEVENTFUL. In all fairness, Jean-François still lingers everywhere. I want to erase all traces of him from my body, and wash him clean from the corners of my heart. I needed to know one good man wants me. Dauro is a gentle man, and his tenderness is tonic for my spirit right now, coaxing flowers to bloom again.

I may, however, not be a woman destined for long-term love. Bob the Hunter, whom I lived with for almost five years when I was nineteen, became so obsessed by his primal instincts that he lost all interest in the romance of our relationship. When he was not hunting, he frittered away much of his time reading *Hunting* and *Field and Stream*, so much so that I contemplated fixing a set of horns on my head to see if that would pique his interest; even his redneck mother sensed the problem, and gifted me a red lace negligee for the cause.

My affection for him faded, especially under the spell of the statuesque cowboys running amok (both urban and real), two-stepping and twirling me around the dance floor each weekend, while Bob sat in tree stands with a bow and arrows, and roamed forests with his guns, stalking innocent prey.

And then there was my too-short-lived marriage.

My fantasies of remarrying have vanished. To have and to hold a man for life seems sadly improbable—it appears not to be the destiny of my life's path, in spite of my crazy love of love, regardless of wishing upon a star every Sunday evening, as Jiminy Cricket urged me to do.

I can only pray lasting love arrives before death.

The windows on the rickety-rack bus bang and rattle as we hurtle down the highway, back to the city from the little surfing town of Sayulita. A young boy in tattered cowboy boots gets on in the middle of a dusty nowhere with a small guitar in hand, and begins to bellow an off-key ballad at the back of the bus. I will give him a good tip for his bravado, but I am tempted to recommend singing lessons. Chuckling, I envision someone getting on a bus in Canada and shouting out a tune at full volume—especially off key. I can imagine the alarm and embarrassment, but here it is a common way to earn pesos. Sellers also deftly hop on and off buses with all manner of treats to fulfill cravings; a wonderful idea in my opinion.

The old-fashioned freedom here is like an unshackling. My father would feel as though he was transported back to Saskatchewan in the '50s, with people riding in the back of pick-up trucks, drinking beer on the bus, parking wherever and whenever you want—the kind of freedom we no longer have.

The noise level here is something one must grow accustomed to: the roosters that crow intermittently all night long; the oom-pa-pa *banda* music blaring wildly at any hour; the rattle-trap cars whizzing by through the night; the raucous *posadas* and festivals are all an assault compared to my sterile, quiet life back home. But now that I have settled into the melody of Mexican life, I have become habituated.

Up late studying Spanish, I had tremendous difficulty yesterday understanding Rodolfo, and I have discovered the source of my confusion. One of my books has completely different phrasing than his. He says most American-published Spanish instruction books have many errors; it is difficult enough for me to grasp the past, present, and future tenses. I will retire the faulty U.S. versions, and stick to the Spanish-produced books. I am an undisciplined student, but I want to do well under Rodolfo's tutelage.

Vivienne's parents are arriving soon, so I have offered to help her and Rodolfo prepare the apartment next door where the couple will be staying. It needs paint and some freshening up. She and I have been going on weekly cappuccino dates, and I thoroughly enjoy her company. Today, she helps translate a letter from Jean-François, so I know it is perfectly decoded into English. He very much wants me to return, and is softer and gentler in his approach with this letter. After reading it, I feel better instead of worse this time, even though it does not motivate me in any way to go back to France.

The barista at the café has gotten to know me and, with a kiss on the cheek, tells me upon leaving that I look better, happier, and prettier each time he sees me.

Sitting at the Burro Bar, Franco drops off my usual mineral water with fresh lime, and compliments me on the green shirt my sister sent in January. The waiters are now used to the fact that I don't drink in the daytime. I face the ocean with my sketchpad and watercolors to paint a simple picture. Playing on the paper, I venture into a meditative state. Afterwards, I open my workbook to write a story for my homework, with Franco checking in to help me with my Spanish.

Running off to see Gina for a manicure, I find her in a Friday kind of mood. I tell her of the characters and their charades on my gay night out at Paco Paco's with Kevin and his friends, and then regale her with the long and crazy tale of last year's reunion in West Hollywood with Wayne and Bruce.

On a scorching night at an outdoor café near the Spanish Steps in Rome, I sat alone, wondering if I had lost my mind, flying off to Italy in the thick of an epic heat wave. Wayne and Bruce sat down at a nearby table while I was contemplating my next move on my last minute vacation. We raised our wine glasses to each other, and they introduced themselves. On a European tour, they were in Rome for four days and, when we parted ways, we agreed to meet the following morning at a Vespa rental place to explore Rome and Trastevere together.

Spending those few days with the twosome was like being in a Seinfeld episode, à la Italy. By nightfall each day, my cheeks hurt from laughing.

A year later, Bruce flew in from England, and I from Canada, for a reunion with Wayne in the *très* gay world of West Hollywood. The first night, I almost came to blows with a striking, but territorial, drag queen at a crammed nightclub. By the end of the evening, I had her singing 'Oh Canada'.

The following night, Wayne pulled off a spectacular surprise party for Bruce and I, complete with a tall, swarthy, well-muscled Italian stripper. The activities of thirty-five raucous gay men— and me—were all captured on Wayne's ever-present video-cam.

Tears roll down Gina's face as I explain that, when stopped at customs in Canada with a video dubbed 'Threesome in L.A.', it was confiscated for viewing. When the customs agent walked off into a private room with my video, I broke into a prolific sweat, so heavy that perspiration ran down my back, pooling in my jeans. Pretending to nonchalantly read a book, it took me five minutes to realize it was upside down. Called into the small interrogation room to explain why I was starring in a video with thirty-five men—one of whom stripped to a full Monty while erotically dancing with me—my stomach violently cramped, and I was certain I was on the verge of something explosively unpleasant.

Maybe I'm still far too much of a wild child to consider settling down again any time soon, and this was all a blessing in disguise.

My sister has arrived. This will be our last, precious visit before she becomes a married woman. She has come at a good time; I have regained sanity, and I am thrilled to see her. However, she has landed in the heat of *Semana Santa*—Easter week. Chaos reigns: makeshift tents are crammed together everywhere, and the beach is teeming with revelers barbequing and building sandcastles. The noise level has escalated to a feverish pitch.

She presents me with a list of things she wants to do on her visit—many are things to prepare for the wedding. I tell her that we don't do lists here—*me*, the Grande Dame of lists. She the turtle, and I the hare, she is confused about what has happened to her Type A, rapid-movement sister.

Since the age of eleven I have worked. I babysat—admittedly not for a love of children, but because it was the only thing anyone would let me do to earn money. The moment I turned fifteen, I applied as a carhopping waitress at the iconic A&W. Working four shifts of eight hours each week, taking up to 250 orders a night while in high school, it was as much as my mother would allow.

For many years, I worked full-time on the road with a massive geographical territory, driving long hours in rain and hail, and plowing through whiteout snowstorms in northern Canada. It never occurred to me to refuse to go because of weather conditions.

Entrepreneurial, I've had side businesses since I was twenty years old and, somehow, convinced the bank to give me a loan for my first gold business at that young age.

Up until three years ago, I designed and made jewelry, often until late into the night, and sold it on evenings and weekends at shows. My current job is demanding, not because of my boss, but because of the scope of duties, with frequent after-hours work (that I opt to do) in my home office.

This is the first time I have ever been on a sabbatical, and I doubt anyone would imagine me taking to Mexican life as I have. An internal-drive switch has been turned off. My body is relaxed and fluid, and my mind has stopped obsessively chasing ideas or issues. The weather has grown more humid and hot, and my pace has slowed to a sensuous rhythm that is unrecognizable.

I have come to the surprising realization that my Type A personality is an aberration of my truest self: it is a maladaptation developed through being 'managed' over the years, with high expectations of myself as a professional; one who must quietly and obediently kiss proverbial ass. I will always be driven by my desires and creative urges, but I now see how delicious a slothful life can be, at least in allotted chunks, such as this one.

Lana and I have been invited to dinner to meet Vivienne's parents who arrived from France a few days ago. I am astonished to find myself attracted to Vivienne's 70-year old father. He is exceptionally handsome—Paul Newman-esque—with a thick head of hair. An uncommon man, he crackles with sensuality. He must have been something in his youth.

Her mother, on the other hand, is the antithesis of her father. Bent and twisted, she exudes an aura of bitterness that saturates the room. Her mouth is frozen in a permanent pucker of dissatisfaction, and she appears as though she is chewing coffee grounds when she speaks. Brusque with her husband, I can only speculate that she has been soured by a lifetime of French infidelity. I'm sure this man has had ample opportunity to participate in illicit affairs.

We mention our day trip to Quimixto and tell them all about the impressive *Semana Santa* displays and altars we passed along our hilly trek. Rodolfo explains the various Easter traditions, and Vivienne's father regales us with tales about life in Provence. Her parents' presence has been helpful, and Vivienne is pleased that Tula has met them so soon. Mother and daughter have cooked a sumptuous French meal, and we all revel in the melding of cultures, here in the magnificence of Mexico.

In the lush, hidden garden of Café des Artistes, Lana and I splurge on brunch. Last night I pulled out all of the paintings I have completed here, the many photographs I have taken on my adventures around the states of Jalisco and Narayit, and the collection of poems I have written in the wee hours. My sister tells me that, more than my new pace, she is most stunned by my swift transition from corporate businesswoman to creative artist.

She comments on the meaning behind each poem and painting. She has noticed my new appreciation of nature, and how I take the time to fully breathe in my surroundings. She is surprised with the ease in which I have embraced the language and people, and how I am exploring each nook and cranny, freely and fearlessly. Even the dresses I have designed for Rosa to tailor are a feminine expression far different from my business life back home.

Lana has seen me execute my career goals with take-charge efficiency, aggressively pursuing achievement, and this new countenance is a previously concealed side of her big sister.

What most astounds *me*, I tell her, is the rapidity with which I have shifted into this converse life. The impulse to strive for goals set by others has dissolved into the Mexican sea breezes. I am comfortable in my body in a new way, because of the amount of healthy movement every day, and my fiery temper has cooled with this unhurried life. This is a newly exposed part of myself that I like, and want to continue to nurture.

After a long day of shopping for wedding fabric and paraphernalia, Lana and I sit at the beach for our last sunset together. Expressing my concerns for my return home, she reminds me that the people who know me hold admiration for my courage to go for my dreams. She gently and wisely tells me that my perspective is tainted by the sudden loss and swift change of plans.

Toasting our last moments before she forges into a new married life, one that I am certain will be busy with childrearing and domestic duties, we linger over margaritas with a light melancholy for the end of an era.

San Cristobal has the best Chiapas beans in town. I stop in for a cappuccino and a home-cooked turkey sandwich, complete with cranberries. Jaime, the man who took me to Christmas mass, waves at me to join him at a cozy corner table. I have not seen him for a long while, and it is apparent he harbors no hard feelings. A turquoise fountain pen I had given him when we met is worn and nearly empty of ink, sitting in this unfortunate state beside his journal. Never have I seen one of my Pilot Pens so thoroughly loved, and I dig another out of my bag to replace it.

We discuss philosophy, and a fascinating book he is currently reading about the Mexican mindset. I show him one of my unfinished Spanish stories, and he patiently corrects it, explaining every error and praising each correct sentence. Then he leaves for work.

Finishing my homework, I detour to a side street to visit Rito, my parrot friend. He climbs onto my arm and investigates my jewelry, buttons, and zipper. We chat in Spanish, and reluctantly, he climbs back onto his perch when it's time for me to go, but then hops down to follow me on foot. I escape into the small store at the next doorway, and find one last donut for later—not a junk food donut, but a fluffy, puffy homemade-like-grandma-used-to-make chewy donut dusted in sugar.

I love Rito. I love this tatty street—every crooked cobblestone, all of the chips and cracks and holes in the sidewalks, and the bewitching house that looks like a stone castle and hides behind a high wall. I love the women who run the tiny *tiendas*, and their toddlers who play on the clay tiles. I love the makeshift taco stands on my route back home, their spicy scents wafting, the sound of sizzling meat as I pass. I love the donkey that lives on the tangled corner lot across from the hotel, and the old man who makes freshly squeezed orange juice each morning on a tiny TV tray outside of his dilapidated doorway.

This place—in absoluteness—holds the frequency of my heart.

May / Mayo

We've got to live, no matter how many skies have fallen.
—D.H. Lawrence, *Lady Chatterley's Lover*

THE WORLD IS LUSH AND RIPE HERE, THE BACKDROP OF THE
Sierra Madres a verdant, tropical green. The heat and humidity
continue to rise, flowers burgeon into gargantuan blossoms, and
the various creepy, crawly creatures are abundant. I have become
accustomed to the crowing roosters on the rooftop next door,
and the barking lizard in my room. I have only a short time left
in paradise.

Stronger now, I have more clarity. A survivor, I have always
managed to pull myself out of life's quagmire of obstacles.

Giving myself permission to leave Canada without a valid
excuse was never a consideration and, with the decision to leave
for love, I have learned something important: I have the strength
to not only survive, but to thrive—in a foreign country, alone.
I have made good friends who may become lifelong comrades.
The classes I have taken, and the people who taught them, have
enriched my experience. Slowly, I am absorbing the nuances of
Spanish, a language I adore. Regaining my sunny self, I am still
able to bring a little light to others, despite arriving in a state of
abject darkness.

The biggest adjustment on my return home will be the
icemen. The smiles, and compliments, and kindnesses that have

watered my withered self-esteem back to life, will dry up and disappear like dust in the wind. Back home, the soured rapport between men and women in my country will, once again, become the bane of my existence.

The barrage of questions I will be asked when I return is not something I look forward to; nevertheless, I feel a pull to get back and regroup—to begin anew. I will reinvent my life in a new city. When we were together, Robert had rightly observed that I am not a suburban girl; I will take his advice and live simplistically in an urban space, with less to manage.

Only months ago, I felt impoverished; I thought I was a woman with nothing. Now, I understand that houses and material things are not what make us who we are, and do not keep us safe or secure. Living 'minimalistically' in a hotel room with few belongings, I have learned something profound: home is wherever I am. I return to little material wealth, yet I have flourished in a way I did not know I could, rising like the Phoenix from bitter ashes.

It is three days before I depart, and I am ever so pleased to have gotten ahold of my friend from those few, riotous days in Rome. With my address book in the trash, I no longer had Wayne's number. After some effort—and a tenacious 411 operator who loved the story—I found him in a suburb of Los Angeles. He is a ray of sunshine, always quick with a witty comment or hilariously acerbic remark. Before I face the music back home, I need to see him. I have arranged for a two-day stopover in Los Angeles. Wayne tells me he has a new Mexican partner, Julio, and that I will love him. Of course I will.

Siting at a serene spot on a picturesque piece of the beach, I meld softly into the moment. I will never tire of a sunset over the ocean. Immeasurable gratitude for the grace of this place envelops me—a place that feels more like home than home.

The first time I came to this country, I was shown extraordinary hospitality and '*mi casa es su casa*' generosity by a family of great wealth. The second time, I was welcomed in a dirt-floor, two-room home, and was proudly offered a fish, the family's only food for the day. This time, I came broken and bereft and was shown kindness, acceptance, and care at every turn. The Mexicans have loved me back to life in a way that would never happen in my own country. The pace and the humanity of this mellow culture have revived my wilted spirit. The sun and the sea have soothed my shattered heart, and brought my body and mind from a state of chaos back into harmony. And I have *played*— possibly the best cure of all.

With reverence, I watch the final tip of the sun sink into the Bay of Banderas. The moment it disappears, a large, black, sparkling butterfly flutters past, and then darts back. She circles me repeatedly, making me giggle. Landing on my arm, she hops onto my outstretched hand, and then softly alights on my cheek, butterfly-kissing me. She stays until darkness settles, encircling me once more, and then she flies off into the night sky.

A tiny angel.

She came to tell me all is as it's meant to be—I will survive.

FIVE

LA VIDA

Twenty-Two Years Later ...

(2019)

Jean-François

Love is so short, forgetting is so long.
—Pablo Neruda, *Love: Ten Poems*

FOR TWO YEARS AFTER I RETURNED TO CANADA, JEAN-François called intermittently. His voice—his French words—would always make my breath catch. And then, the memories would rush in, and remind me. Each time, he would ask me to return to France, and every time I would ask, *"what for?"*

In the middle of a sentence one night, on a call in the wee hours, I ripped the phone cord out of the wall, its box of wires dangling as though in a daze. I was finished. There was nothing more to say.

He stopped calling.

♥

Ten years later.

I had just completed my manuscript of *The Cuban Chronicles*, my first travel memoir. Two years earlier, my intention had been to go to Oaxaca, Mexico, for a month's sabbatical in the fall, to begin writing *Fragments of French*. As fate would have it, a political upheaval erupted, days before I was about to leave for Mexico. Making a sudden detour, an offer I couldn't refuse came up for Cuba.

On the sultry streets of Havana, I met a spicy *cubano* journalist.

Caught up in the sensual vibes of the Cuban music, the culture, and the heady amorousness of a witty and handsome local (who, in a sardonic twist, reminded me in so many ways of Jean-François), the book writing was abandoned.

I did, however, outline my Cuban adventure in a 33-page letter to Monique, who was still in France. Upon learning of my tryst, friends suggested I write a book about it. Returning for a Cuban Christmas rendezvous with Paulo, the journalist, I promised that I would write a book if I had enough juicy content. As it went, I had plenty of scandalous material for a romantic misadventure and, so, I completed that book first.

The sunny day I sat at my computer after the Cuban manuscript was completed, and in the hands of the editor, is etched in my brain. Itching to get back to my original project (this book), I was at the first phase of outlining and sketching the timelines of my neglected tale. Jotting notes, I was interrupted by a random thought to check my travelogue. Only occasionally receiving messages from readers, I hadn't visited it for many months. A single notification was flagged at the inbox and, when I clicked on the email, my heart seemingly stopped beating.

MESSAGE: Jean-François Boulanger.

Unsteady on the edge of my chair, I tottered, pushing down on 'open.'

> *Bonjour Wanda,*
> *Do you remember me? Jean-François Boulanger. I am very sorry for our story ten years ago in Lisbon. Many times I tried to find you, but I was unsure if it was a good*

idea. Please let me know how you are. Are you married? Children?

I await your reply.

Did I remember him? My head swirled in a spin. *Did I remember the most monumental event of my lifetime?* I was on the verge of writing an entire book about it. Knee-jerk, my response was an abrupt and unedited letter in return.

In 2010, I received a phone call from a woman speaking French in an accent remarkably similar to Jean-François. Asking if I spoke the language, she gave up when she realized my ability was limited. I always wondered if she had found my phone number in his things.

The following year, an ongoing series of letters arrived. It had been fifteen years since our love story in Lisbon, but I remained in Jean-François' mind.

I have always loved you; you were the ideal woman for me. You left footprints on my heart, and I regret not having you at my side for all of these years.

He remembered me as ambitious, and a woman of strong character and courage—unafraid of life. He told me of his life, and that he was to retire in a year, but more than anything, he wanted to apologize for breaking my heart.

Laying the groundwork for a possible reunion, letters kept coming. In one, he outlined a proposal for us to meet. So many years since Portugal, my mind wandered tenuously into the closed-door section of my life. Was this fated? What would happen if we met again? Would we see each other, the years falling away, the spark reignited? Or would we look at each other and wonder why we had such strong recollections of an outrageous love?

With an imminent retirement, he offered to send me a ticket to France for a rendezvous at his country home. I knew I required neutral ground; venturing into his territory after all of these years was inappropriate for an initial meeting. Secondly, the letters outlined his desires and goals, yet oddly there were no queries about mine—nothing that indicated my wishes or dreams would be a part of the plan. If he was showing no consideration for my needs—especially in light of the transgression years earlier—how did a reunion bode for me?

No matter my curiosity, and the temptation to see him again, I came to the conclusion that it was a risk I was not willing to take. The consequences had proved to be too far reaching the first time. But further to that, I was a different woman. He could not have tamed me years ago; single and free for so long, any illusions of domesticating me were foolish.

We were just not meant to be.

In 1991, scientists discovered 40,000 specialized cells in the human heart—brain cells that think independently of the cerebral cortex. Emotions that we store in our brains are also warehoused as memory in our hearts, not metaphorically, as we have always been lead to believe, but literally.

Many years after France, I saw the movie *Love in the Time of Cholera*, and thought the plot was a sad testament to love—and somewhat implausible. Almost absurd. The protagonist, Florentino Ariza, falls in love with Fermina Daza. Her father disapproves, moving her to another city to end the romance. The two stay in touch, but eventually, she lets go of her first love and meets a doctor, whom she marries. In spite of her nuptials, Florentino vows to stay faithful and wait for her. Promiscuous, he has many dalliances, but his heart remains in limbo for Fermina for over fifty years.

December 23, 2016, I sat at Roberto's Café patio in Puerto Vallarta, writing and listening to the ocean crash the shoreline. Like a rogue wave, it struck me that it had been exactly *twenty years* since I had come from France to Vallarta to heal. Roberto's had not existed then, but I had sat at that same spot many times on my 'historic' stay. With regret, I realized I was, in a peculiar way, similar to Florentino. My heart, in a manner of speaking, had remained in limbo.

Less than an hour after my recollection of Florentino and Fermina, and recognizing the juxtaposition of France, my email pinged. A note from Jean-François shocked me out of my reverie.

> *Bonjour Wanda,*
> *Je te souhaite un Joyeux Noël et une bonne fête de fin d'année, aussi et avant tout une très bonne santé.*
> *Je t'embrasse,*
> *Jean-François*

This message led us to a long-overdue healing moment.

We began a dialogue. He still held deep shame for what had happened between us. He asked for, and needed, my forgiveness. Not only considering what I would write that would absolve him, I also spent quiet time sending him the energy of my forgiveness; I hoped for him to *feel* it.

Dear Jean-François,

I write to let you know you are forgiven. It is myself that I have been unable to forgive, but now, I feel that I finally do. I chose my perceptions and subsequent actions.

Shame and guilt are destructive, and twenty years is so very long to carry them. Please let them go. It is time. It is amazing that events can scar us for so long—unbelievably long—but this is life on Earth. However, we have the freedom to release the pain, and we both deserve it.

You are in a well-earned retirement after an extensive and hard work-life. I truly wish you joy and happiness. Also liberation in mind, body, and soul.

Be well.

Jean-François still sends a note each New Year. And he knows of this book. Should he find the courage to read it (as he said he would), the accuracy of the smallest details will likely surprise him. I kept copies of every letter he sent, each fax and letter I sent and received from everyone, and all of my journals. Also, I have powerful recollection.

In response to his annual letter last year, I asked Jean-François if he had found a partner to spend his retirement with. Reluctantly, he revealed he had met a woman who lives with him in his country home, and that they travel extensively. A small part of me mourned the final closure—the shutting of the door. A tiny piece of me, I discovered, still harbored a misty fairytale fantasy of him as a knight who would one day rescue me from loveless-ness. The small girl inside of me still wished upon a star.

I hold no regret for meeting Jean-François. Many will never experience the type of romance and love I did on that fateful trip to Portugal. Some things, I believe, are fated. I am a woman who prefers life when it's large. Jean-François was a big personality, our love story brief, yet grand.

Après

> "Hearts are breakable," Isabelle said. "And I think even when you heal, you're never what you were before."
> —Cassandra Clare, *City of Fallen Angels*

I CAME TO EARTH FERVENTLY BELIEVING IN MAGIC. WHEN I was a child, I was convinced I could fly, and appointed my mother Master Wing Maker. Together, we tried every construct of design imaginable to a five year old; the operation was shut down after I attempted to fly down the stairs with a set of spectacular wings—which I was certain would ultimately render me airborne—but instead landed me in a badly bruised heap on the bottom step.

Bewitched and *I Dream of Genie* mesmerized me, and I was captivated by the idea of creating the unexpected from a secret power within.

Many years later, on that fateful day when I met Jean-François on a bustling street in Lisbon, every part of my being felt as though I had finally entered the sparkling doorway to a magical world that I knew existed. The wild love and crazy laughter I had dreamt of as a young girl was made manifest, and I took flight.

Alas, when you fly too close to the dazzling sun, you run the risk of scorching your wings. Falling from that exhilarating high can land you in a shadowy, cold place. The enchanted kingdom I thought I had discovered turned into a landmine to circumnavigate.

When my French love adventure tumbled sideways, I knew something had profoundly shifted. What I could not know was how that fracture would affect the next twenty-plus years of my life: the good, the bad, and much in between.

The meaning we attach to the events of our lives, as I have come to learn, determines the outcomes in front of us. Dr. Robert Anthony states, "*The problem with perception is that it not only influences the way things were, and the way things are, but the way things will be in the future.*"

Instead of viewing the French fiasco as another '*c'est la vie*' chapter in the book of my life, I bore the experience as the ultimate rejection. Pinning all of my hopes for a new life, and new love, on one man—that dream came crashing down like dominoes, in the blink of an eye. The rebuff saturated every cell of my being and, oh so gradually, eroded my sense of self-worth.

I did not mean to do it. I did not purposefully construct it. Perhaps it emerged as I flew away from the border of France, leaving him for the last time. Possibly, it happened the moment when I sat on my luggage on the streets of Paris and wept. Or maybe it took seed later, in Mexico, while mired in my grief. But at some point, far in the recesses of my subconscious, I drew a line in the sand. Without my conscious consent, my subconscious mind made a subversive decision to never be that vulnerable again—to be hyper-vigilant to the wolves of the world. I lost my trust in men, but more grievously, I lost trust in myself. And when you don't trust yourself, you trust nothing. With that line as a foundation, I built a castle—a fortress, if you will—around my heart.

With such a resolution, the ego believes it is defending you, keeping you safe from further harm; it is looking after your best interests. Unfortunately, it does not have the capability of discerning how intensely such armor affects every aspect of life. It may protect, but it also powerfully deflects. It resists joy to avoid pain.

Had I observed my misguided conclusions with more aware-ness, I would have seen the monumental turning point I was creating. I allowed that one event to radically alter the landscape of my heart.

The years after France have been a mélange of extremes. I traveled solo to exciting places, such as Cuba and Argentina, and I returned to Mexico many times, occasionally for months at a time.

My life became deeply enriched by culture, language, music, and Latin dance. I painted emotive pictures, I wrote real and raw stories, and I photographed my experiences with an eye for capturing people and things worthy of note.

I dated exotic, larger-than-life men, like the virile Italian baritone opera singer from New York, and the stunningly gifted Mexican musician who looked like a regal Apache Indian, and had the temperament of a shaman.

The greatest goodness that was born from my 'love story gone bad' was how it became the catalyst to unlocking what laid dormant within, the key to the epiphany from that moment when a stranger in Italy prompted the soul-reveal that I was an authoress—traveling incognito. Had I not experienced the pain, I don't know if I would have been compelled to put pen to paper, fingers to keyboard.

Writing became a cherished friend and intriguing compan-ion. It nudged and persuaded me to do what I thought I could not. Words became my fundamental *raison d'être*. Still, this story took so very long to write.

Upon my return to Canada in 1997, I jumped back into my sales life in earnest, but at the same time, brainstormed on my first writing project, and created a series of gift books called the *Circle of Life*.

Within a year, my super-boss, Ron, decided to step away from the business and into retirement, leaving it in the hands of his son and his curmudgeonly partner. With the loss of his leadership—and with my risk-taking spirit still intact—I left my job two years after returning to Canada to launch the series, and leapt into a writing life.

Pre-France, my life was abundant: I had a cozy home of my own; I stayed in luxurious hotels and ate at lavish restaurants for business; I traveled as I wished, and prosperity circulated without thought or effort. But my world was self-centric.

Post-France, the girl who'd landed in Lisbon on that warm summer's eve was exponentially expanding her experience in the world, and learning to love in a much broader way.

But life also brought more misfortune and strife. Even with extreme effort and persistence, bolstered by the guidance of wise advisors, my small writing business suffered financial devastation. I was forced to return to a long-term sentence in a corporate sales life, one that felt like the tethering and breaking of a wild horse.

Though roped and tied, it couldn't keep me from writing. In high spirits after successfully launching *The Cuban Chronicles*, I elatedly planned a 'celebration of life' trip to Italy. Two *amigas* who had beaten cancer were going to commemorate the victory with a long-dreamed-of excursion to the land of *La Dolce Vita*.

But once again, destiny had something else in mind. Two weeks after Lynnette and I booked the flight, I found a lump in my other breast. It was a devastating blow; I had lost a twenty-year triumph over cancer. Everything was upended, and all writing came to a halt.

After the second diagnosis, I sank deeper into reflection, and researched the biggest question of my existence: why do we get the results we get in our lives, be they pleasant or poor? I spent long hours studying the psychology of illness and of wellness. In light of my broken spirit, I learned that a return of cancer was not such a mystery, after all.

Five years later, on a chilly November morning, the Universe delivered an unambiguous message: I was under order to share all that I had learned, even though I'd had no prior interest in revisiting all the emotions that would come through writing about cancer. Despite my stubborn resistance to take on such a serious and heavy task, I eventually acquiesced. Again, my French story was waylaid by a soul calling to write an entirely different type of book.

Once I made the commitment to give as much to the project as I had in me, I was still, at times, baffled about why I was writing the book *(What To Do After "I'm Sorry, It's Cancer")*. I wasn't an expert or a doctor. However, by the time I completed the manuscript, a mission was made manifest to offer the book as my legacy of service to the world. When emails started to arrive, and people called to tell me their stories after reading the book, I understood that my unique perspective of the cancer journey, and the retelling and distillation of what I had learned, had validity. I knew exactly why I had written it.

After creating, conceiving, and birthing that book, I returned to my European love story in earnest—the one I most wanted to write.

The ending—the denouement—however, became the grand block.

I considered a delightful French-themed fall launch but, through spring and into summer, I was stymied by what I had wished for all along—a happy ending. By the time the manuscript went to press, I wanted an honest, swear-to-tell-the-truth-and-nothing-but-the-truth-so-help-me-God happy ending. No matter which way I looked at my life, I could find none.

Enter autumn. Not a typical red-leafed and yellow-hued fall, but a rude thud into a sunless, snowy-winter bypass. Another Groundhog Day season in a place—and in work—that did not feed any part of my soul, seemed unbearable. With an extremely early winter, depression threatened to engulf and overwhelm me. I knew what to do—I had many tools—but, like an addict, I was repeatedly ambushed by my attachment to a history of defeat.

For what felt like an eternity, I had been trapped in the stage of the Groundhog Day story where Bill Murray imagines that he's in purgatory, caught in a never-ending loop, in an icy Punxsutawney, with the same cast of characters.

The Heart Restored

Don't worry if people think you're crazy. You are crazy. You have that kind of intoxicating insanity that lets other people dream outside of the lines and become who they're destined to be.
—Jennifer Elisabeth, *Born Ready: Unleash Your Inner Dream Girl*

THE HERO'S JOURNEY IS THE NARRATIVE OF *ALL* LIVES, NOT just the characters of our favorite stories or mythical legends. As Joseph Campbell told us, the journey begins with our ordinary lives.

Next, is separation; a call to adventure, with an offer to leave whatever space or place we are in, whether internal or external. Fate summons the hero; we can refuse the call, or step into something that will turn our lives upside down, and potentially change everything we know to be true.

If we refuse, because the call is too risky, we may find ourselves in stagnation, with a sense of dissatisfaction. If we cross the threshold, life will never be the same as before.

After that, is initiation. There will be tests and trials, challenge and crisis. This stage of conflict pushes us to acquire strength, and offers us the opportunity to find our own authentic path, veering away from the hypnotic highway of the masses.

Dragons must be slayed. We may descend into hell, fighting with our life, to find the treasure.

An inevitable death occurs; old ways, beliefs, a relationship, a career, or a way of living, must die. We may hit rock bottom. Without death there is no transformation; without death, no resurrection.

Everything we hold precious—and our very survival—may be laid on the line. We hit a do-or-die moment.

If we cross the finish line intact, we find the treasure or elixir. It can come in the form of the material, of love, or of new wisdom and knowledge. We seize the reward.

Returning to the ordinary world, we leave the extraordinary behind, victoriously possessing the prize, which can then be used to improve our lives. We come back to tell our story, with the gift of impacting others in a meaningful way.

The journey is cyclic, with the call showing up throughout our lives in different forms, repeating again and again if we do not heed its message.

In the dead of that Punxsutawney winter, I went away for a Christmas holiday to escape the doldrums. Once back into the melody of Mexico, magic happened. Love rushed in to meet me from the most unexpected places, and nature salved my ennui. With more fervor than ever, I wanted to stay. Inspired, I worked to finish my French book. Still, I had no ending for it.

A week before I left Mexico, two "prophetic" things occurred. My editor asked me what was next, after this book. I had tossed around the idea of an experiment: a year of making the impossible possible. With my love of magic, manifestation, and miracles, it sounded like a playful and fun project. If I could live it and track it, I could write about it and share it.

Also, a friend I was staying with wanted me to watch a Ted

Talk about designing your life. She had been motivated by the message, and we agreed to do an exercise set forth in it. The speaker said that he frequently challenges clients and students with the task. He asks people to envision three different lives.

A) Whatever you're doing, keep doing it. It's going to turn out great. But make it better and add some bucket list events.

B) What you are currently doing becomes obsolete. You are not needed anymore. As of tomorrow. What will you do?

C) A wild card plan. You've got enough money to do what you want. No one will laugh or think you're crazy. You don't care what anyone thinks. What amazing things will you pursue?

We told each other our A plans. Next, she told me her B plan. She had various creative ideas. When she asked me for me B plan, I had none, so we moved onto C.

A wild card plan? Now we were talking. I knew exactly what I'd do with a C plan—the key factor being that I had the means to do what I desired.

Unsatisfied with my exclusion, she backtracked.

"So, what's your B?"

"I don't have a B."

"You have to. Would you ..." She set forth to list a multitude of ideas.

I said no to all of them.

"Well, what would you do then?"

"There is no plan B. I have an A. And I'd love the C. But, *there is no B*."

"You have to have a B," she stated.

"Well, I don't. I have no idea what I would do if my job disappeared and I had to move forward with no means. My plan is to go from A to C when it comes together. I'm really, really tired of all the B plans. They are over."

Flummoxed, she let it go.

Returning home with a revived heart, I could not have imagined that my hero's journey was about to bring a harsh, wildly ironic call. Literally minutes after I got off the airplane on a Sunday evening, I learned that my six-year-long position had been eliminated. Effective immediately. Hearing those words, I felt myself falling from a cliff. Echoes of plan B slammed into my brain.

"You are obsolete. As of tomorrow."

Working at both the sensible sales career while writing at the same time, my plan all along had been to go from there, into my creative life full-time—when I was in the position to do so. I'd had no intentions of starting over at this stage in life; of learning a legion of things I had no interest in, of kissing more managerial butt, of doing something I hated for a pay cheque.

This was *not* a plan C; with no net, the news plunged me into a void.

Having been through countless tests, I had a pattern; I fell hard, and then quickly regrouped, planned, and executed.

Not this time.

With this unforeseen—and umpteenth—shockwave, my normal resilience shattered. I questioned my value and my existence. The irony of the map of unhappiness I had drafted, and the painful thoughts that I didn't belong here, was in essence, that I loved life and planet Earth too big and too much to continue living in a cage.

I committed heresy; *all* logic dictated I march forward with an intense job search. Yet no part of me would do it. If there was anything I had learned from writing my cancer book, it was that stress and unhappiness triggered disease. The insidiousness of ignoring one's authentic self was the most harmful threat to wellness.

Life had been generous; I had survived divorce and infidelity, major back surgery, France, two rounds of financial devastation, dastardly employers and soul-sucking jobs, displacement in an epic flood, an insane menopause, and cancer *twice*—and I was still standing. How long would life keep showing me beneficent grace? Was I going to wait for a *third* cancer to give myself permission to live authentically? Did I need a death sentence before I would show myself the love and compassion that I gave to others?

Twenty-two years earlier, I had discovered who I really was, and what I so loved. Every position and side job I had taken since was born from fear. And not a single one was fulfilling, had healed my finances, or brought me to my dreams. If I chose, yet again, to ignore the message and continue to betray my truth, I knew in my heart that I was very likely headed down a perilous path.

This was the point in the hero's journey where my survival was on the line. It was time for a true surrender. Even though the road ahead appeared to be hazy and treacherous, I exhumed every ounce of trust, from every pore.

The surprisingly poignant themes in the animated film *Moana* have stuck with me, and came to the forefront of my mind. The key thematic element is that of being true to oneself. No matter Moana's predestined role in her tribe, the sea keeps calling her. In spite of continual warnings and threats, she ventures out to find the heart of Te Fiti, the goddess who created life. Because of Moana's courage and dedication to her mission (to save the islands and, in turn, humanity), the sea steps in to aid her in moments of need and danger.

The dramatic scene where Moana fearlessly faces the fiery and ferocious Te Kā struck me most. Painfully evident was the powerful metaphor, that when we allow our hearts to be 'stolen,' a stony shell encrusts everything, cutting off the nourishment for life to thrive. When we restore the heart to its rightful state, verdancy and abundance can spring forth in a stunning rapidity (Te Fiti restored).

In the years since France, I had too often viewed my 'island' as largely withered and parched. When I assented to surrender, flouting logic, I stepped back to view the foliage. From a bird's eye view, I saw that it was not a dead garden. Yes, there were weeds and wilted flowers. But there was an abundance of growth—different from the tropical jungle that burgeoned in Portugal—yet filled with a splendid array of color and variety.

However, the dragon to be slayed on my hero's journey was still hiding in the garden behind the florae and, like the ireful Te Kā (who, in actuality, is Te Fiti)—she was *me*. Once called out from her dark cave for a faceoff, she was as incensed and retaliatory as Te Kā. In command of the garden for perpetuity, she would not so easily be relegated to bystander.

The fight against my inner enemy was fierce. She wanted to hear nothing of forgiveness and kindheartedness towards my mistakes. While I examined my life with more generous and gentler eyes, she, in turn, dragged me through the garden, pointing out the dead underbrush and the flowers that lay on the ground, lifeless and withered. She roared in convincing indignation; how she had become so powerful was painfully vague. With weary doggedness, I continued to rise while under attack, but by all appearances, the dragon wished me dead.

Moana sweetly sings to a rageful Te Kā, "*He may have stolen the heart from inside you. But this does not define you.*" In spite of the fury directed at her, Moana confronts Te Kā with love and understanding. The moment Moana restores the heart of

Te Fiti/Te Kā, the magnificent goddess with the power to create life emerges, her lava shell cracking and falling away, the island springing into lush, fertile life. (Moana Restores the Heart of Te Fiti: https://tinyurl.com/yxz6rkp9)

As with Moana versus Te Kā, buckling under the tyranny of my inner dragon would mean defeat. Yet fighting against such a formidable foe was not only exhausting, it was a war of one-step-forward, two-steps-back. I was either going to win this battle and manifest a new and authentic life, recklessly flee the country with nothing and burn all bridges, or die.

I needed to mirror Moana's stance. In order to have harmony and renewed growth in the garden, I had to restore the heart of the angry dragon with empathy and love. Dismissing the struggle for dominance, I invited the dragon to a peaceful truce. What we had not understood was that, without one, we could *both* perish.

Instead of focusing on the footprints of failures and wrongs, I asked her to take a closer look, and see not only the setbacks, but also the successes. I hadn't hit society's view of victory, but I had created many things that had left a positive, ripple effect in the world. I did not have a partner, but I had compassion, and the love that I gave came back to me from unusual and astonishing sources, in a multitude of ways. My life, in spite of strife, was filled with serendipity and synchronicity, and 'impossible' things had been made manifest. Courageously, I had picked myself up with each knock, regenerating, and reinventing myself anew, rather than giving up. I asked the dragon to see how all of these things, blended, had given me (us) a resilient richness and depth of being.

The time had come for the cruel creature to stop making me wrong for being different, for having opposing desires and predilections to the status quo. I asked her to stop forcing me into a restrictive prison, letting me out on leave now and then for good behavior, because incarceration had never proved rehabilitative. I presented to her the repetitive and now siren-level warning call of my journey: *to thine ownself be true.*

Alas, we came to a critical armistice. Where the dragon thought I was straying off course was, in fact, the path into the unknown and higher plan of my soul.

Years ago in Portugal, I sought a big romance—and made a resounding declaration that I wished for a man who would 'rock my world.' The prayer I had asked for in my afternoon meditation in Lisbon was answered; my world *was* rocked. And just as Te Kā let go of her story of pain, the one shaped by the feckless Maui who had stolen her heart, I could release the stories that had taken root and propagated since the Frenchman.

The hero's elixir I fought so hard for was far greater than romantic, singular love—a highly conditional love, which can evaporate overnight, as though it never was. The treasure I thought I had found in Portugal was infinitesimal, comparatively. This elixir had the power to create life. This was the true Holy Grail—it was a radical act of self-love to stop imprisoning myself with work that brought me no joy or satisfaction.

I was finally un-breaking my own heart. My hero's journey led me to the most important love of all, with myself as the savior.

Unbridled

As I began to love myself, I quit stealing my own time, and I stopped designing huge projects for the future. Today, I only do what brings me joy and happiness, things I love to do and that make my heart cheer, and I do them in my own way and in my own rhythm. Today, I call it "simplicity."
—Charlie Chaplin

MY INTENSE COMMITMENT TO SET MY HEART FREE—TO HEAL it at last—set me free. This winding, arduous journey has lead me back to my true self, my little 'magician of the beautiful,' who once believed in the benevolence of the Universe.

We are the creators. This planet is a dense, difficult speck in the cosmos, this much I know is true. But it is also an illusory dream (or nightmare), and again, as the J Man told us when he performed miracles, *these things and more you can do*. We have the power to select a potential that already exists in the fabric of divinity.

When I declared to life that I wanted 2019 to be a year of making the impossible possible, it knew that I could never do so from my Groundhog Day existence. It knew that without a profound push off of the perch, nothing bold or bodacious could manifest.

Joseph Campbell famously stated, *"Follow your bliss and the Universe will open doors for you where there were only walls."*

When I, alas, heeded the call to lay my very survival on the line for my bliss, doors began to slowly open, where previously I saw no way out. Love allowed me to move from stagnant survival to emergent creation.

At the outset, this could have appeared to be just another travel tale of a wanton woman on a misadventure. My impetus goes far beyond entertainment; my ardent wish is that in the sharing of this messy, beautiful journey, you will be inspired to let go of old stories that bind you; that you too will set yourself free from any chains that hold you from your soul's spectacular plan.

People will say you are wrong for loving what you love. Do not let them stop you from the life you came to live, no matter what place they hold. If you harbor any trace of bitterness; if your heart has become jaded by life—but especially if you know that you have forsaken yourself—let this raw, cautionary tale gently incite you to heal the hardened fragments back to the soft vulnerability you began life with.

Now, I am able to close my book and lay this story to rest. Finally, I can finish my tale of a most unexpected journey of the heart—maybe not with the "happy" ending I wanted for myself, and for you the reader. Although in its infancy, I *can* leave you with the knowledge that I have been freed into a rebirth, where I can explore, expand, and enlighten, as I was always meant to do. Once the truce was made with the dragon, and I summoned my inner reserves once again, I committed wholeheartedly to "a write life"—my right life.

I *can* plant the seed that it's never too late to become who you are meant to be, even if you have walked a long journey through the halls of hell.

In the land where my soul flutters with felicity (Mexico), the resplendent Quetzal flies as a symbol of liberty, reminding me that, I too, am at last liberated from the false prison I unconsciously created.

Honor yourself like your life depends on it.

Because it does.

Cast of Characters

Adriana and Samuel: Now the matriarch of Paloma del Mar, Adriana divorced her husband a few years after my original stay. As I suspected, Samuel (the owner of Paloma del Mar), was in love with her. Eventually, he pursued her, and they married. They have one son who, at the time of publication, is a teenager.

I have stayed at the hotel many times since the French fiasco, and Adriana watched out for me when I lived there on a one-month pre-surgery cancer treatment trip.

After learning Samuel has early onset Alzheimer's, I visited the hotel recently. My heart burst when he recognized me and, in that moment, I realized how much these two souls have meant to me on this journey.

Annette: Rita's travel friend, Annette, still stays at Paloma del Mar on vacations, and has become close friends with Adriana over the years. I see her at dinner parties and gatherings.

Beto: I ran into Beto one month ago in Mexico. He drives a taxi, and still loves beer more than sobriety.

Bruce: The last time I saw Australian-turned-British Bruce was on a two-day layover in London on my way to Greece many years ago. He looks fabulously GQ, and is a successful businessman living in Monaco. We're Facebook friends.

Dad: Remaining a bachelor since he and my mum divorced, dad is youthful, and an ever-sharp philosopher who questions *everything* about life. Afraid of flying, we have yet to get him out of Canada. I'm quite certain he's still trying to understand his black sheep daughter (hint: it's not my sister).

Darren: My baby brother returned from the Land Down Under (shocking us all with long hair), and buckled down as a serious engineer. He got married, and he and his wife, Carlene, adopted two sets of high-energy twins from Haiti. The 'A twins' are now 19 years old, and the 'J twins' are 13 years old. All four kids are award-winning athletes, and my brother and his wife have a hectic domestic life.

Dauro: Two years after my stay in Mexico during the French fiasco, I returned for another four-month writing sabbatical in Vallarta, and rented an adorable little pink house I called Casa Rosita. In a desperate attempt to repair a botched haircut (I'd asked for Meg Ryan, and instead got Dudley Moore), I went to see Dauro at his salon. He had met a Mexican girl, they'd married, and she was pregnant. That was the last time I saw sweet Dauro. He may have returned to Italy with his new family.

Delores: Delores and I are still in touch via Facebook and email. She spent some time living on the Caribbean coast of Mexico, and is a successful realtor in Edmonton.

Donna: My nurse friend surprised everyone (especially me) by taking a contract in the Middle East many years ago. There, she met an American military man, whom she fell in love with. They married and she, most fortunately, escaped the cold. They are happily retired in Florida, and we keep in touch.

Gina: My manicurist still lives in Mexico, and we have remained friends throughout the years. I have had many opportunities to see her (my last trip to Mexico was my forty-seventh). She had three wonderful children; one wild-child beach boy, Emylio, one sweet baby girl, Aryana, who unexpectedly left us after only 8 months of life, and a future famous artist girl, Aliyah, who is the most enthusiastic Christmas gift-giver I have ever known.

Gina owns a large, lovely home, and a bustling and successful salon in Bucerias.

Jaime: I saw Jaime on my trip the following year of this story, but have never had a sighting since.

Katarina: Eventually, Katarina left her sullen young husband. She still lives between Santa Maria and Canada. We have remained friends, mostly via email, and I last saw her on my après cancer trip in Vallarta in 2010, when she came to stay with me in a house on a hill where I recovered, surrounded by nature—with a lot of roosters.

Lana: My sister got pregnant the night of her wedding. Literally. (The minute I saw her I knew it; a case of sister's intuition.) She had two blonde boys, both of whom I helped birth into the world. Each extremely bright, the talkative 21 year old is in university studying to become a lawyer, and the quiet 18 year old is a hockey superstar.

Lana's marriage played out worse than I had predicted. Thankfully, she ended it—after much adieu. She lives and works in the magnificent Okanagan Valley in British Columbia.

Lynnette: Lynnette, my other nurse friend and dear soul sister, saw me through two breast cancer experiences with tender loving care. Much to my sadness, she was diagnosed years later with breast cancer, and last year (2018) we lost her. My cancer book is dedicated to her, and I am happy she got to read it. She valiantly fought the disease, and went through her journey with far more grace and humor than I *ever* could. I so much wanted for her to read this story, because she was an integral part of that period of my life. If you're reading this from another dimension, Lynnette, I miss you and love you.

Lynn: Even though I sometimes expect her to disappear into the ether, she's still around. She and the clingy Pablo ended their relationship, but have stayed friends. She has reinvented herself, and morphed many times since we met in Mexico.

Monique: Much to my dismay, Monique came back to Canada to live. Because it suited her so very well, I envisioned her living in Paris for the rest of her life. Having returned to care for her failing mother, and staying to be close to family, she lives in Edmonton with a precious cat named Lizzie. We have remained cherished friends, and she is still as beautiful and chic as the day I met her thirty-four years ago.

Mum: My mum is still with the man she met soon after her divorce. In her late 70s, she stays active as a professional face painter, and plays Mrs. Claus at Christmastime. She and her husband, Mich, live in Edmonton, and spend winters in my Mexico, where she vigilantly dodges the geckos that terrify her.

Pepe: Casa de la Salsa stayed in business for many years. It recently changed hands and is operating under a new name since Pepe retired. I am forever grateful to him and his boys for seeing me through a difficult time.

Rita: I spent only a brief moment in Mexico with Rita, but when I moved to Calgary, après France, we became partners in crime, dancing our weekends away at Don Quixote's, a popular salsa nightclub. We are dear friends, and she has always been my biggest writing fan and supporter. She has *never* doubted my future bestseller status as an author. I know no one more generous than this feisty little dove of love.

Rodolfo, Vivienne, baby Tula, and Chou Chou: Vivienne got pregnant again, making the baby Rodolfo's 14th child at 67 years of age.

Vivienne opened a tranquil Euro-styled café with lots of books and classical-only music. She made delectable French treats and good coffee and it was an ambient place to relax and read.

Unfortunately, most tourists weren't looking for that.

Seeking a better life, Rodolfo and Vivienne made the decision to move to France. I have not heard from them since. I hold tremendous gratitude in my heart, and will never forget how they welcomed me into their lives with such love and generosity.

Ron: I will always consider Ron Pirie the best boss in the world. The respect and rewards he bestowed on me were a rare gift in an oftentimes-viperous business world. In my search to find him to gift him this book, I was deeply saddened to learn that he died suddenly on April 12th, 2016. I was gladdened to know he had been living in Ajijic, Mexico, and that his wife Elda and daughter Kim, both of whom I worked with, were by his side when he passed. Thankfully, I found Elda, and she will receive a copy of the book. I love you, Ron.

Shari: My soul-sister bestie and I have seen each other through countless ups and downs since we were two-stepping, wild-assed urban cowgirls at 19 years old. She owns a hugely successful dance studio in Edmonton, and the secret to her endless energy and tenacity remains a mystery. A BFF, she's a supportive and loving friend to the very end.

Susan: Susan went on to become a sales manager in our industry, and then moved on to bigger and better things in British Columbia.

Teresa: Reconnecting two years ago in Mexico after a long separation, it felt as though it had been a month's gap. Teresa remarried and is living a good life in Edmonton. A new fan of my writing, I sincerely hope she enjoys this tale, as retold in far greater detail than the story she knew of at the time.

Terry: Today, as I wrote this cast of characters, I received a Valentine's Day text from my ex-husband. Last year, on a trip to Los Angeles, my sister and I met with him to spend a day in

Venice Beach. He had married a lovely American woman and she had, sorrowfully, just passed away. He is working his way toward retirement in Mexico. I wish the very best for him.

Wayne: My comedic friend from my Italian vacation stayed in touch, and we had a riotous visit on one of my stays in Vallarta. After that, we lost contact for a number of years and reconnected on Facebook.

On the trip my sister and I took to Los Angeles for a weekend event with Kyle Cease, we met up with Wayne for an outrageous dinner at 'lifestyles of the rich' Nobu in Malibu, where we had a Sam Elliott sighting, and ate Drake's favorite tempura crab dish.

Wayne is tamer than our wild '90s days, but still travels a lot and gets up to a more laid back, domesticated type of trouble.

Language Glossary

abuelas (Spanish) – grandmothers

à cause de toi (French) – because of you

adios (Spanish) – good-bye

agua de Jamaica (Spanish) – water infused with hibiscus leaves

amigas (Spanish) – friends (female)

amour extraordinaire (French) – extraordinary love

après (French) – after

arrêt (French) – stop

au contraire, monsieur (French) – on the contrary, sir

aujourd'hui nous sommes samedi et c'est notre dernier ... (French) – today is Saturday and it is our last ...

Au nom du Père, et du Fils, et du Saint-Esprit. (French) – In the name of the Father, and the Son, and the Holy Spirit (the sign of the cross).

au buerre (French) – with butter

arrivederci (Italian) – good-bye

arrondissement (French) – a city district

babushka (Russian origin) – kerchief to cover the hair

bacalhau (Portuguese) – single most important dish in Portugal—dried salted cod

banda (Spanish) – a style of raucous Mexican music; country, ballads, boleros

barrio (Spanish) – neighborhood

birria (Spanish) – spicy beef stew originating in Jalisco, Mexico

caipirinha (Portuguese) – national drink of Brazil

cerveza (Spanish) – beer

c'est la vie (French) – such is life

claro que sí (Spanish) – (clearly, yes, is the literal translation) certainly, yes, emphatically

déplacements (French) – displacements to other locations for work

el centro (Spanish and Portuguese) – the center of the city

escudo (Portuguese) – Portuguese currency of 1996

Fado (Portuguese) – literally means destiny/fate; Fado is a traditional form of melancholic and mournful music of Portugal

faire l'amour (French) – make love

feliz cumpleaños (Spanish) – happy birthday

fêtes (French) – parties

gentil (French) – kind, friendly, good, pretty

grand-mère (French) – grandmother

gracias (Spanish) – thank you

gracias á ti (Spanish) – thank you to you (literal) it is a response to being thanked—thank you

Guadalupana (Spanish) – song for the religious patroness of Latin America, the Virgin of Guadalupe

hay algún recados? (Spanish) – are there any messages?

huevos (Spanish) – literally, eggs, figuratively, testicles

imitation peixe (French) – imitation fish (JF blended French with Portuguese word for fish)

incroyable (French) – incredible

Je suis malade. Complètement malade. (French) – I am sick. Completely sick.

je t'aime (French) – I love you

je t'embrasse (French) – I kiss you

joie de vivre (French) – joy of life

Jesus Cristo (Spanish) – Jesus Christ

la dulce vida (Spanish) – the sweet life (Italian version: *la dolce vita*)

la madrugada (Spanish) – dawn, the wee hours

l'amour existe encore (French) – love still exists

la petite mort (French) – the little death—orgasm

la princesa (Spanish) – the princess

Las Mañanitas (Spanish) – Mexican version of 'Happy Birthday'

lavandería (Spanish) – laundry

le Français (French) – the Frenchman

ma chère (to a woman/French) – my dear

mais non! (French) – but no!

malecón (Spanish) – pier/seawall

mamma mia (Italian) – literally, my mother, used to denote "wow!"

maseca (Spanish) – corn flour

mercados (Spanish) – market shops

merci (French) – thank you

mère (French) – mother

Mexicanos (Spanish) – Mexicans

Mexique (French) – Mexico

mi casa es su casa (Spanish) – my house is your house

milagros (Spanish) – miracles, also, religious charms

moi aussi (French) – me too

momentito (Spanish) – tiny moment

mon amour (French) – my love

mon Dieu (French) – my God

non (French) – no

obrigado (Portuguese) – thank you

osso buco (Italian) – braised veal

pain au chocolat (French) – bread with chocolate, croissant style pastry

palapas (Spanish) – thatched sunshade

pardon? (French) – pardon?

pâtisserie (French) – pastry shop

pensão (Portuguese) small hotel or boarding house

pension (French/European term) – small hotel or boarding house

pensione (*Italian*) small hotel or boarding house

père (French) – father

petiscos (Portuguese) – gourmet snacks; comes from the verb petiscar: to eat a little of this and that

piri-piri (Portuguese) – spicy sauce or style of chicken

"*Parlez-vous français, mademoiselle?*" (French) "Do you speak French, miss?"

si (Spanish, Portuguese) – yes

poco a poco (Spanish) – bit by bit

panga (Spanish) – modest fishing boat

posadas (Spanish) – advent celebrations (also has a meaning of: inns)

pozole (Spanish) – traditional Mexican soup with hominy and pork

raison d'être (French) – purpose, reason for being

segunda (Spanish) – a secret second 'wife' who is not married to a man

Semana Santa (Spanish) – Easter, literal: week of the saints

s'il vous plaît—maintenant (French) – please—now

sooky-faced (Wanda-ism from friend Donna Z.) – miserable, pouty face

sola, sola en el olvido (Spanish) – ... Alone, alone in oblivion (sola – a feminine of solo)

sola con su espíritu (Spanish) – ... Alone with her spirit

sola (Spanish) – ... Alone

tagliatelle (Italian) – a broad pasta noodle

tamale (Spanish) – steamed corn husk or banana leaf filled with corn meal and various fillings

tchotchkes (Yiddish, Slavic in origin) – Sentimental trinkets or miscellaneous items

tiendas (Spanish) – shops

tomatillos (Spanish) – green-husked type of tomato used for green salsa (nightshade)

tout de suite (French) – right now

très (French) – very

tres leches (Spanish) – delicious white sponge cake made with three types of milk

tu me manques (French) – I miss you, which literally translates to 'you are missing from me'

Un petit peu (French) – a little

Oui. Mais oui. (French) – Yes. But yes.

vinho tinto (Portuguese) – red wine

vinho verde (Portuguese) – 'green' (young) wine from the Minho region of Portugal

viva l'amor! (German song) – Long live love! (from Julio Iglesias song: Bravo, E Viva L'amor)

voilà! (French) – there you are/there it is! (expression of satisfaction)

Bonjour Wanda,
Je te souhaite un Joyeux Noël et une bonne fête de fin d'année,
aussi et avant tout une très bonne santé.
Je t'embrasse,

Hello Wanda,
I wish you a merry Christmas and a Happy New Year, and above all very good health.
I kiss you.

Merci

A pocketful of thanks to Marie Beswick-Arthur, my editor/confidante, and Richard Beswick-Arthur, proofreader and fact checker extraordinaire. To Ryan Fitzgerald, my designer/technical guy, thank you for your expertise at helping me birth another book into the world. To my sister Lana—my brilliant beta reader—cheers to you for your attention to detail, and to Marilyn, for your final proof.

Thank you Dianne Quinton, for your unwavering dedication to my dreams—for keeping me on track with my writing and my purpose for so long (I appreciate it to the end of time), and to Christine Brennan, for helping get me through to the book's finish line.

Francis, thank you for the gorgeous and evocative cover photograph.

Thank you David, the marketing monk, for your incredible generosity of time and knowledge. You're proof that serendipity and magic both exist.

My immense gratitude to my family and friends, for your belief in me, and for your profound support during the 'French Fiasco' period of my life, so many years ago. I love you all very much.

To my sweet baristas at Kawa Espresso Bar and El Café de Bucerias, *gracias* for the many fab lattes I consumed while writing this book.

Merci beaucoup, to you, my reader, for traveling far and away with me on this unexpected journey of the heart.

About the Author

Her prime passion is the thrill of travel—of experiencing other cultures, traditions, lifestyles, and languages—thus expanding her perspective.

Wanda St. Hilaire has a predilection and passion for all things Latin, and she believes life is too short not to do what you love, where you love. She spends time writing in Mexico for inspiration, and to escape the frozen landscapes of Alberta.

Through writing, St. Hilaire shares what she's learned from the high peaks of adventure and love, to the dark valleys of illness and heartbreak. Her mission is to help people overcome the self, and tap into their wise inner guidance system. Her wish is to inspire others to live true to their unique and beautiful nature.

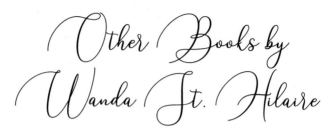

Other Books by Wanda St. Hilaire

Of Love, Life, and Journeys
(Companion Poetry Book to Fragments of French)

The Cuban Chronicles, A True Tale of Rascals, Rogues, and Romance

What To Do After "I'm sorry, it's cancer." An Exceptional Guidebook for Navigating Your Way to Health and Happiness

Circle of Life Series (small gift books)

Websites
www.wandasthilaire.com
www.imsorryitscancer.com
www.fragmentsoffrench.com
https://www.etsy.com/ca/shop/LittleEtsyBookstore
(Circle of Life series)
Blog: www.lifebyheart.wandasthilaire.com

Workshop
Impossible Things Happen Every Day

Contact
destinoex@aol.com

Books to incite impassioned odysseys through life